GRAMMA NANCY'S
animal hats
(AND BOOTIES, TOO!)

Knitted Gifts for Babies and Children

GRAMMA NANCY'S
animal hats
(AND BOOTIES, TOO!)

NANCY NIELSEN
Foreword by Vanna White

POTTER CRAFT

NEW YORK

Published in the United States by Potter Craft, an imprint
of the Crown Publishing Group, a division of Random
House LLC, a Penguin Random House Company, New York.
www.crownpublishing.com
www.pottercraft.com

POTTER CRAFT and colophon are registered trademarks
of Random House LLC.

Library of Congress Cataloging-in-Publication Data
Nielsen, Nancy.
  Gramma Nancy's animal hats (and booties, too!): knitted
gifts for babies and children/by Nancy Nielsen; foreword
by Vanna White.—First edition.
     pages   cm
  Includes index.
1. Knitting—Patterns. 2. Children's clothing. 3. Infants'
clothing. I. Title. II. Title: Animal hats, and booties, too!
  TT825.N54 2014
  746.43'2—dc23   2013048518

ISBN 978-0-8041-8519-6
eBook ISBN 978-0-8041-8520-2

Printed in China

Design by Rae Ann Spitzenberger
Photography by Heather Weston
Set styling by Kimberly Rygiel

The author and publisher would like to thank the Craft
Yarn Council of America for providing the yarn weight
icons used in this book. For more information, please visit
www.YarnStandards.com.

10 9 8 7 6 5 4 3 2 1

First Edition

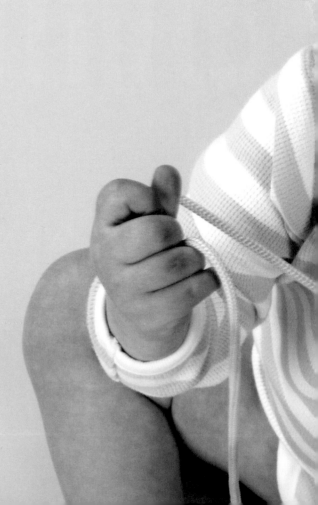

This book is dedicated to the *families* of those who serve in the armed forces, who are never thanked enough.

And to my husband, Hans Peter Nielsen, who holds my heart in his hands, and without whose whole-hearted support, you would not be holding this book in yours.

contents

FOREST FAVORITES

BEAR 38

BEAVER 44

FOX 50

OWL 56

RABBIT 62

TOAD 68

JUNGLE JUBILEE

MONKEY 76

FISH 82

LION 88

ELEPHANT 96

PANDA 104

TURTLE 110

BARNYARD BUDDIES

CAT 118

CHICKEN 124

BLUEBIRD 128

DOG 130

DUCK 136

LAMB 140

PIG 146

foreword

BY VANNA WHITE

I was absolutely thrilled when Nancy asked me to write a few words introducing her first book. I truly love creating gifts with yarn, and I am always excited to see someone else expressing the same passion.

Nancy and I first met at the 2013 Craft & Hobby Association's trade show in Anaheim, California, where she was awarded Grand Prize in my Vanna's Choice Contest, hosted by the Lion Brand Yarn Company. Not only did the judges at Lion Brand and I love her whimsical hat and bootie creations, but they were also the most popular designs with everyone else who stopped by our booth that day.

Many great designs were entered into the contest, but something stood out about Nancy's patterns. Her animals have details that are so original and realistic yet also fun. Little did I know at the time that there was a great story behind these delightful designs, too.

Nancy's motivation for knitting was to support her daughter, who is married to a Command Master Chief, at that time responsible for 150 men aboard the USS *Alabama,* a naval submarine. The couple was looking for a way to provide special gifts, on a budget, to welcome the new additions to all the crew's families.

When her daughter turned to her for help, Nancy realized that she had the skills to create baby hats and booties that cost more in creativity and time than money. As all of us who knit or crochet know, there is nothing more special, and more appreciated, than giving something handmade that comes from the heart.

To create unique gifts, Nancy developed more and more patterns, until she had a whole menagerie of animals, discovering her talent for designing along the way. She has touched the hearts of hundreds of people at a special time in their lives, and supported the families of

people who serve our country. When it came time to enter my contest, Nancy had an army (and a navy) of grateful recipients from around the world to support her. What a great example of the amazing things that can happen when you live generously! That's why I'm so proud of Nancy and so delighted to finally see her wonderful Gramminals collected in this book.

I hope you'll enjoy Nancy's designs as much as I do and wish that you'll have many happy occasions to make them for loved ones.

And, when you do, please use my Vanna's Choice yarns. Lion Brand Yarn Company donates a portion of the purchase price to St. Jude Children's Research Hospital for every skein you buy. Since 2007, Lion Brand has donated over $1 million to this important cause.

Vanna White

introduction

It all started in 2010, when my son-in-law became the COB (chief of the boat) of the Navy submarine USS *Alabama* and was made the senior enlisted adviser of some 150 sailors of the Blue Crew. So many sailors! So many young families! So many new babies! I wanted to support those families without breaking the bank and began knitting hats to give to my daughter, Jessica (the COB's wife), to gift as the occasion arose.

When I volunteered to "whip up" a bunch of baby hats for my daughter to give away, out came four love-worn patterns that I had bought in the late 1990s. They included an assortment of fruit-shaped hats, which served as my introduction to the magic of circular needles, textural stitches, two-color knitting, and other methods that helped me think outside the box when I later started to design. I'll never forget how impressed my then ten-year-old grandson, Bradley, was when he saw a pumpkin hat I had just finished. "You *made* this?" he exclaimed incredulously. I explained that I had knitted it, and while I was showing him the needles and the yarns I had used, he interrupted me. "Wait a minute," he said, shaking his head vigorously. And then, holding the hat in one hand and squeezing a skein of yarn in his other hand, he squealed, "You mean you made *this* out of *this*?"

I followed those four patterns for a couple of months before I started modifying them, starting with the pumpkin hat. It needed a different color stem and, come to think of it, it needed a pumpkin leaf and tendrils. An online search turned up a lot of not-so-good-looking samples, and even more blog entries of people asking, "Does anyone have a good pumpkin leaf pattern?" Over the next few days, I printed out a pile of patterns and knitted up a heap of not-quite-right leaves, until I was informed enough to produce one of my own that pleased me. And, in that passionate pursuit of the perfect pumpkin leaf, I awakened my long-dormant, joyful obsession with design. Who knew?

Early on, my daughter, Jessica, pointed out that the fruit hats I was making were pretty much for baby girls. She suggested that I start thinking about designs that were more appropriate for boys, saying, "I don't know, Mom, maybe you can make some kind of animal."

Her suggestion led me to the world's best website, www.lionbrand.com. There I found and printed out a pattern for the Baby Animal "Froggy" Hat and knitted up a few to resounding applause. Not being able to leave well enough alone, however, the Froggy became a Toad when I added bumps and modified the crown and eyes, and then I designed the most delightful webbed-feet booties, creating my first complete ensemble.

I've knitted many generations of each animal you'll find in this book, continually perfecting each one. And, as the months passed into years, my love of design grew, and my body of work grew into a whole kingdom of critters that I call "Gramminals," animal hats with matching booties and mitts, or handsies. Hundreds of Gramminals, knit with my own two hands, have found happy homes all around the world. Not only do they live in many places all across the United States, from Oahu to Boston, but they have traveled far and wide to Canada, China, New Zealand, Africa, Australia, and the Netherlands.

Sadly, there aren't enough days in a lifetime to knit a Gramminal for every baby who should have one (God knows, I've tried!), so now it is up to you. My patterns are tried and tried and tried, so you can follow them with complete confidence and a joyful heart.

It is my dream, one day, to be shopping in the grocery store and notice one of my hats on the head of some little darling sitting in a shopping cart. When I do, I'm going to ask their mother, "Where did you get that hat?"

And, when she says, "I made it myself," I'm going to ask, "Was it hard?"

And, when she says, "Not at all. It was fun," I'm going to be the happiest Gramma in the whole, wide world.

xoxo,

Gramma Nancy

May your labor of love
make you ever-so-proud.
And make your little ones
laugh out loud.

A LABOR OF LOVE

>>>

TOOLS & MATERIALS

As a knitter, you will be familiar with most of the items I use, but you might notice a few surprises here that are entirely unique to my designs. I'll introduce you to the inexpensive items and time-saving techniques I use to make these projects.

1. Medium- (or worsted-) weight acrylic yarn
2. US size 8 (5mm) 16" (40.5cm) circular needle
3. Set of 5 US size 8 (5mm) double-pointed needles
4. Stitch marker
5. Large-eyed blunt-end yarn needle
6. Size F-5 (3.75mm) or G-6 (4mm) crochet hook
7. Scissors
8. Measuring tape or ruler
9. Stitch holder or a large safety pin
10. Round and egg-shaped Styrofoam balls (cut with a bread knife or other serrated kitchen knife)
11. Plastic animal eyes
12. Plastic black doll eyes
13. Plastic animal noses
14. Pink acrylic paint
15. Clear nail polish
16. Side-cutting needle-nosed pliers
17. Felt, for tongues and paw pads
18. Polyester fiberfill
19. Round glass bowl vases
20. High-heat (60-watt) hot-glue gun and glue sticks

Premium Acrylic Yarn

When knitted hats and booties started leaving my house at the pace of two sets per week, the challenge was to make a keepsake baby gift as inexpensively as possible. To that end, I limited myself to yarns that were under five dollars per skein and found a large selection at Michaels and Jo-Ann Fabric and Craft Stores. Starting at the lowest price, I tested and eliminated the yarns that were too stiff and scratchy for a newborn, or too limp and lifeless for a hat, or too thin for the size 8 needles I was using (the ones I already owned). Vanna's Choice yarn had the soft, springy stretchiness I was looking for and, because of its rich body and thickness, finished up beautifully on my needles. I signed up for sale notices and only shopped on discount days, dragging my husband with me to spend two 50 percent—off coupons. A single skein of Vanna's Choice yarn is enough to make two newborn hats and a pair of booties, or two pairs of booties and one hat, so I could make three complete sets with two skeins of yarn for a total of four dollars. Fan-frugal-tastic!

High-Temperature Hot-Glue Gun

I love to knit, but I don't like to futz with sewing things together, and because I am a bit of a perfectionist, I am never happy with the way my sewn stitches look on my finished projects. Therefore, no-sew assembly is an integral element of these designs. The ears are knitted directly onto my hats (the Lamb being the only exception), and all of the other bits and pieces, from faces to fins and flippers, have been designed to look like they were sewn on expertly, even though they are intended to be attached with hot glue.

I only use plastic eyes, and since acrylic yarn is a form of plastic, too, a very hot (at least 60-watt) glue gun bonds the two surfaces together. My young moms report that, years later, after a lot of wear by both their first- and second-born children, those eyes are still on the first hats I ever made. If you glue your eyes on askew, there is no fixing them later. (Believe me, I have tried.) So, make sure you have five minutes, all to yourself, to focus on assembly before you heat up your glue gun.

If you have more patience and skill than I do, of course you can sew each piece onto the hat, hiding your stitches on the knitted ledge under it (where I run a bead of hot glue). If you are a purist, or are using

» All of the hats in this book can be washed in cold water and laid flat to dry. Avoid heat if your hat is assembled with hot glue or Styrofoam.

nonacrylic yarn, instead of gluing on plastic eyes, you may choose to embroider eyes with scraps of yarn or to create them with shapes cut from felt, as I sometimes do. See the Fox (page 50) and the Owl (page 56) for two examples.

Styrofoam Snouts

Budget-friendly Styrofoam, cut with a serrated knife to the patterns' specifications, provides lightweight shaping for snouts, cheeks, and hoofs. These components are knitted separately, and then hot-glued together first into a face. Then the whole face piece is hot-glued directly onto the hat, exactly where it's supposed to be.

Plastic Animal Noses

The noses I use come with posts on the back of them that fit easily into Cheeks. To fit the post into a Snout that is filled with Styrofoam, however, you'll first need to make a hole in the center of the snout, using a double-pointed needle. Always make certain that you put hot glue on the yarn of the knitted Snout, not just in the hole. Gluing the post to the Styrofoam will not give you a secure bond. You must run your glue around the hole, to be sure that your hot glue bonds the yarn to the back of the nose. (Plastic animal eyes often come with posts, too, but they are snipped off with side-cutting needle-nosed pliers before being glued in place.)

If desired, paint the nose pink with acrylic paint and add a shiny top coat of clear nail polish before attaching it to the hat. See the Rabbit (page 62) and the Cat (page 118) for two examples.

Round Glass Bowl Vases

To complete a hat, I always use one of several glass bowl, or bubble, vases, which I found in the flower-arranging department of my local craft store. With three sizes—15½" (39.5cm), 17" (43cm), and 18½" (47cm) in circumference—you'll be prepared to finish any size hat in this book. Dried hot glue has no stretch to it, so it's best to glue details to a hat in its stretched form. When the hat is stretched on a round form, it looks just like it's going to look on your little one's head, making it obvious where the snout and eyes should be. And best of all? Hot glue does not stick to glass!

ABBREVIATIONS

My smart, sophisticated, successful, lifelong friend Paula, who loves to knit—and knits a lot—insists that she *just can't* follow a knitting pattern. She says they intimidate her, so she pretty much limits herself to scarves and pot holders. My BFF with a BA is stupefied by a puny, little *psso* and an even-smaller *ssk*. LOL!

To make it easy on yourself, here is the very short list of each and every abbreviation used in this book. For more comprehensive information on these techniques, turn to Knitting Essentials (page 150). Whether you are being introduced to a new stitch or just need to refresh your memory, there is enough information shown in the illustrations there either to get you started or to keep you going.

*	Repeat steps from or between asterisks
k	Knit
k2tog	Knit 2 together (decrease)
k3tog	Knit 3 together (decrease)
kfb	Knit front & back in same stitch (increase)
ktbl	Knit through back of loop
M1	Make 1 stitch on bar between needles (increase)
M1P	Make 1 purl on bar between needles (increase)
p	Purl
p2tog	Purl 2 together (decrease)
psso	Pass slipped stitch over (decrease)
RS	Right side of work (knit side in stockinette stitch)
sl 1	Slip 1 stitch from left needle to right needle
skp	Slip 1, knit 1, pass slipped stitch over (decrease)
ssk	Slip, slip, knit (decrease)
WS	Wrong side of work (purl side in stockinette stitch)

THE METHOD TO MY MAGIC

In the creative process, I have made many missteps and met many maddening design issues that I resolved by using some very old and some entirely new techniques. Many of my methods will be familiar to you, as they have been around a long time. Others are unique to my designs.

Knit Cast-On

It is essential that you use the *knit cast-on* to start a hat, booties, and handsies. This method creates a row of actual knit stitches on the left needle and has hardly any stretch in it, which provides a better, tighter roll on the Rolled-Brim Hat (page 28). The knit cast-on also provides a proper start to the garter stitch border for the Earflap Hat (page 30), and it creates a more seamless join between the flaps and the finished hat. The knit cast-on is also essential when knitting most components that are made separately and attached to the hat later.

Create a slipknot on the left needle, and *insert the tip of the right needle as if to knit. Wrap the working yarn around the tip of the right needle, draw the right needle through, and place the newly created loop on the left needle. Repeat from * until the number of stitches indicated in the pattern has been cast on. With the knit cast-on, the working yarn ends up at the beginning of the left needle, ready to knit the first row without turning.

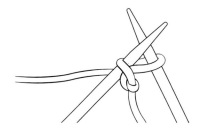

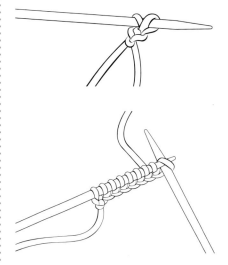

If the pattern instructions do not specify using a knit cast-on, feel free to use the cast-on method of your choice. Or, you may simply use the knit cast-on for all cast-on instructions.

Circular Knitting

Before beginning to work in the round, I work *1 row flat*, with the yarn ending up on the right needle, ready for joining, with plenty of available stretch to do so. Use a 16" (40.5cm) circular needle for this step.

To join the knit stitches to work in the round, hold the needle with the working yarn in your right (or dominant) hand, place a stitch marker on the right needle, and knit the first stitch off the left needle. Continue knitting in a circle, noting that the stitch marker indicates the end of each round.

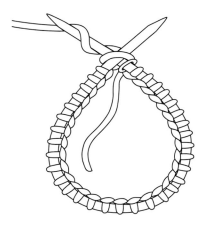

Knitting in the Round, on Two Double-Pointed Needles

Ears, most pieces and parts, booties, and handsies are all worked in the round, but stitches are divided between just two needles: a front needle and a back needle, which are knit or purled with a third working needle. The stitches on the back needle always mirror the stitches on the front needle, which means that they are worked in *backward order* from the front needle, thereby reversing shaping. To keep things straight, there is a semicolon placed between the instructions for the front needle and the instructions for the back needle for each round. And, after each increase or decrease round, you are given the total number of stitches followed by the breakdown of the number of stitches on each of your front and back needles.

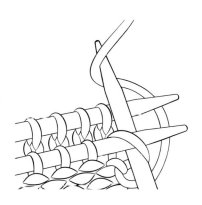

Picking Up Stitches for Ears

If you are a better knitter than I am, you may be able to pick up the stitches for the front needle of your ears, using a double-pointed needle to begin with, but I find it is much easier to start them off on a crochet hook, and then to transfer them onto a double-pointed needle afterward.

To start, find where you will begin the first stitch by counting to the left

from the center "wheel" at the top of the hat. Using a crochet hook (I use a size F-5 [3.75mm]), push the crochet hook under the entire V of the stitch (both bars) and pull yarn from under and toward you, creating a stitch on the hook.

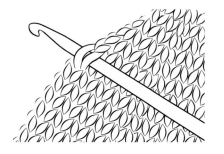

Go under the next V (in the round below) and pull up another stitch onto the crochet hook. Continue in this manner, pulling up stitches, until you have picked up all the stitches the pattern requires.

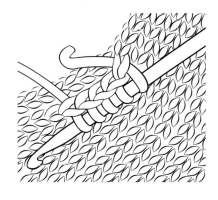

Transfer these stitches onto a US size 8 (5mm) double-pointed needle. Then flip the hat over and pick up another set of corresponding stitches

on the back side of the hat, in the row right next to the ones already placed on the first needle. You don't need to transfer the second set of stitches onto a second double-pointed needle; simply knit them off of the crochet hook on the first round. If you've done this right, when you look down between your needle and hook, you will see the two rows of knit Vs that you used.

Long Cast-On Tails

After you have finished knitting a hat component, you may be instructed to use the cast-on tail for finishing. Pay particular attention to the length required so that you will have the right amount to finish the piece without needing a new strand of yarn.

Creating a Flat Ledge

Many components need to be finished with a flat ledge underneath them, before they are attached to the hat. This flat ledge is made possible by creating a bend in your work by knitting the first row *flat*. After you knit 1 *row*, you will turn your double-pointed needle to the purl side when you begin knitting in the *round*. This bend in your work is required to enclose Styrofoam pieces into snouts and to finish components that are stuffed with fiberfill, creating a flat ledge, where you can apply hot glue and give the appearance that it was sewn on.

Some facial features (including beaks, cheeks, jaws, and nose triangles) don't need a ledge, so you will join your knitting to work in the round right after the knitted cast-on.

Long Ending Tails

Some bootie (and handsie) patterns require using a long length of yarn to simultaneously close up gaps and continue knitting. After finishing the first toe (or finger opening), measure and cut the tail to the length instructed.

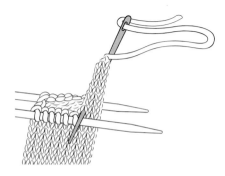

Continue knitting the rest of the toes using this tail, after first sewing a few stitches across the gap between toes and finger openings. Thread the tail down through the toe, coming out the bottom stitch at the inside edge of the toe. Sew into the next lower stitch and come out the same (adjacent) stitch on the needle in the back. Sew under the back bar and out the adjacent front bar. Sew

into the stitch under the first stitch on the needle in the front and under and out the adjacent stitch on the needle in the back.

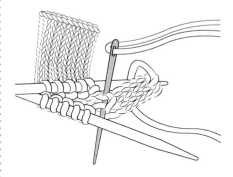

You are now ready to knit again (with the long tail) on the needle to the left of the finished toe, with the yarn coming from the back. Now you are assured that there will be no gaps between the toes.

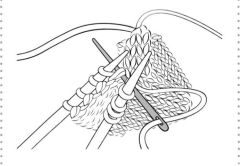

Stitching a Mouth

To stitch a mouth, I start and finish in the same place so that I can tie the beginning and ending tails together, where the knot will be hidden under the plastic nose. Beginning at the center of the mouth, where the plastic nose will be secured, sew straight stitches out to the corner of one side of the mouth, leaving equal spaces between the stitches. Then, sew back toward the center, filling in the spaces with straight stitches on the way back, and ending in the same place as you started.

ASSEMBLING A FACE

Individual facial features, such as snouts, cheeks, and jaws, are first knitted, then shaped, and finally glued in one piece to the main body of the hat. These photos will show you step by step how some of the basic components are formed and assembled, but always refer to your pattern for specific instructions.

SIMPLE SNOUTS

1. Thread the cast-on tail onto a blunt-end needle and hold the snout with the purl side facing you. Sew into the bars of the cast-on edge by inserting the needle under the first bar from the outside and pulling the yarn through.

2. Once you have sewn through approximately half of the cast-on bars, place the Styrofoam ball into the center of the purl side of the nose and pull the tail until it starts closing around the ball.

3. Sew through the rest of the bars, tightening stitches as you go. Weave in the end.

4. Stitch the mouth as the pattern directs, beginning and ending the line of stitching in the center of the snout, where the nose will hide the knot.

NOSE TRIANGLES

1. Thread the cast-on tail onto a blunt-end needle and hold the piece with the purl side facing you. Sew only into the bars of the cast-on edge, going under the first bar from the outside and pulling yarn through.

2. Tighten stitches as you go until you have sewn through all the cast-on bars. Pull tightly and weave in the end.

JAWS

1. Thread the cast-on tail onto a blunt-end needle, and hold the jaw with the purl side facing you. Sew only into the bars of the cast-on edge by inserting the needle under the first bar from the outside and pulling the yarn through.

2. When you are finished sewing through all of the cast-on bars, pull yarn tightly, creating a disk. Weave in ends.

CHEEKS

1. Thread the cast-on tail onto a blunt-end needle. Sew across the bound-off edge by inserting the needle under each bar *between* the purl bumps at the top, from the outside. Sew into the bars of the cast-on edge only by inserting the needle under the bars from the outside.

2. After sewing through a few of the cast-on bars, place two Styrofoam pieces side by side in the center of the wrong side. Pull the yarn tight to enclose. Finish sewing through the remaining cast-on bars, tightening as you go. Sew across the top again, ending in the middle.

3. Create definition between the bottom of the cheeks by bringing the cast-on tail down the back side and up in front between the cheeks, sewing it through to the back side, just below where the nose will be.

4. Tie the beginning and ending tails together in a double knot behind the cheeks and trim the ends. Add other details, such as a nose triangle or jaw, according to the pattern.

BEAKS AND BILLS

1. Thread the cast-on tail onto a blunt-end needle and hold with the purl side facing you. Sew only into the bars of the cast-on edge, going under the first bar from the outside and pulling the yarn through.

2. Once you have sewn though about 10 cast-on bars, tighten the yarn, gathering the edges enough to begin shaping the beak or bill.

3. When all of the cast-on bars have been sewn through and you are happy with the overall shape, pinch the sides together to create a prominent ridge in the middle of the top and underside of the piece.

4. Weave in the end. For the Owl (page 56), the pattern instructs you to combine a top beak and bottom beak, as shown above.

LONG SNOUTS

1. Thread the cast-on tail onto a blunt-end needle and hold the knit snout so you are looking inside of it. Sew through the bars of the cast-on edge, under the first bar from the outside, and tighten until all the cast-on bars have been sewn through.

2. Pull tightly to form the snout shape and to create a nice, finished edge on the front and a flat ledge underneath that will easily attach to the hat. Weave in end.

3. Hot-glue a plastic nose between the finished cheeks. Hot-glue a felt tongue to the jaw, and hot-glue the jaw behind the cheeks. Hot-glue the bottom half of this whole piece to the bottom of the finished end of the Snout; at first, it will look too small to fit.

4. Stretch the top of the Snout to fit into the cheeks, and hot-glue it in place. Fully stuff the Snout with fiberfill.

GAUGE & FIT

If you use size 8 needles and a yarn of the same weight as Vanna's Choice, you don't need to take extraordinary measures to ensure that your knitting gauge matches mine. Even if you knit a little tighter or looser than I do, you'll have splendid results using my recommended materials.

Gauge

You'll notice the symbol (4) listed after each yarn in the pattern's Materials list. It describes the weight, or thickness, of the yarn according to the Craft Yarn Council's Standard Weight System. Medium 4 yarns, (also known as medium- or worsted-weight), however, are not all alike! My preferred yarn, Lion Brand Yarn Vanna's Choice, is the thickest yarn made that still falls in the Medium 4 category. And, because I use one-size-smaller needles than those recommended on this yarn's label, my gauge is different than what is shown on the label. If you choose to use different materials than the pattern recommends, please knit up a quick gauge swatch to check that your combination of yarn, needles, and your own personal gauge matches mine—16 stitches and 24 rows over a 4" (10cm) square of stockinette stitch (knitting on the right side and purling on the wrong side.)

Hat Fit

On average, my Newborn size fits from birth to six months, Small from three months to eighteen months, Medium from twelve months to seven years, and Large size from five to ten years.

But not all babies are the same! Your child's age does not necessarily tell you which size hat size will fit them. Heads come in an incredibly wide range of sizes at every stage of life. I have made a Medium-size hat for both nine-*month*-old Sofie and nine-*year*-old M'lynn, both girls with head sizes considered normal for their age. I kid you not.

Each hat pattern is offered in four sizes, stepping up ever so gradually, so there is a hat size that will fit your little one from the happy day they are born until the sad day they tell you (in no uncertain terms) that they are way too old for Gramminals. Girls enjoy them well into their tweens, however, and I am happy to report that I made a Panda for Joey, a very cool sixteen-year-old boy, who wears his to school!

Bootie Fit

Each booties pattern is offered in only three sizes: Newborn, Small, and Medium, since they are intended to fit babies only through their first year of life, or until the day they start toddling, whichever comes first. Because they are designed to finish on the long side of average, if your baby has an itty-bitty foot, there will be extra length after the toes, but it is so much better to have

room to grow into a bootie than for it to start out too small. There is just enough length on the leg of the bootie to hold on to your baby's calf, which is what will keep the bootie on. Kneesock-length booties are hilarious, especially on birds and webbed-footed ducks and frogs. You can make them as long as you want simply by starting with more rounds before you get to the heel flap.

Handsie Fit

There is something particularly funny about little paws and claws on a newborn baby's hands, since they always seem to hold their hands up high around their faces. My thumbless mitts, or "handsies" for newborns, whip up in two-thirds the time that it takes to make a pair of booties, and they use two-thirds the amount of yarn. You can make handsies instead of the booties, or if you have the time and ambition, you can go all out and make a complete set for a four-legged animal. You will find the newborn handsie pattern following the bootie pattern for each Gramminal except for the Elephant:

we wouldn't want our newborns to hit themselves on the head with the Elephant's foot!

Older kids also love a matching pair of animal handsies, so I designed an option for their busy lives that leaves their fingers free (page 32). Children's hand sizes are even more wide-ranging than their head sizes, but fingerless handsies only need to fit around the palm. That way, each size fits for a goodly amount of time.

BASIC PATTERNS

The following patterns are the blank canvases for your little works of art. Choose from two hat styles, which are used as the starting point for many of the animals, and a fingerless handsie pattern that can be used to complete a Gramminal set for older children. Both hats are very easy to make and fit snugly against the crown of your little one's head, so that the ears perk up properly, with a nice, flat finish at the top.

rolled-brim hat

Easily knit in the round, this style of hat fits the greatest range of head sizes for the longest amount of time and can be used for most of the projects in this book. Because yarn has a wonderfully stretchy quality, each size hat will stretch more than 2" (5cm) in circumference. The thick brim will unroll as needed to fit your growing baby's head.

sizes
Newborn (Small, Medium, Large)

finished measurements
13½–16 (15½–18, 17½–20, 19½–22)" (34.5–40.5 [39.5–45.5, 44.5–51, 49.5–56]cm) maximum stretched circumference

gauge
16 stitches and 24 rows = 4" (10cm) in stockinette stitch

materials
47 (59, 71, 85) yd (43 [54, 65, 78]m) / 1 ball Lion Brand Yarn Vanna's Choice, 100% premium acrylic, 3½ oz (100g), 170 yd (156m), in desired color (4)

US size 8 (5mm) 16" (40.5cm) circular needle, or size needed to obtain gauge

Set of 5 US size 8 (5mm) double-pointed needles, or size needed to obtain gauge

Stitch marker

Blunt-end yarn needle

INSTRUCTIONS

With circular needle, knit cast on 54 (60, 66, 72) stitches. Do not join.

Note: Knit cast-on instructions are given on page 20.

Knit 1 row flat.

Place marker and join to work in the round, being careful not to twist stitches.

Work in stockinette stitch (knit every round) for 27 (31, 35, 39) rounds.

SHAPE CROWN

Note: Switch to double-pointed needles when necessary.

Round 1: *K4, k2tog; repeat from * 9 (10, 11, 12) times—45 (50, 55, 60) stitches.

Rounds 2 and 3: Knit.

Round 4: *K3, k2tog; repeat from * 9 (10, 11, 12) times—36 (40, 44, 48) stitches.

Rounds 5 and 6: Knit.

Round 7: *K2, k2tog; repeat from *
9 (10, 11, 12) times—27 (30, 33, 36)
stitches.

Round 8: Knit.

Round 9: K2tog 13 (15, 16, 18) times,
k1 (0, 1, 0)—14 (15, 17, 18) stitches.

Round 10: K2tog 7 (7, 8, 9) times, k0
(1, 1, 0)—7 (8, 9, 9) stitches.

FINISH
Cut yarn, leaving a tail for closing.
With blunt-end yarn needle, thread
tail through the remaining stitches.
Pull tightly and weave in end.

earflap hat

This hat style will also fit through more than 2" (5cm) of head growth while continuing to fit snugly against the top of the head, allowing the Gramminal's ears to stand up properly. As your baby's head grows, the brim of the hat will creep higher and higher up the forehead. Nevertheless, the garter stitch flaps on either side will keep their little ears warm.

sizes
Newborn (Small, Medium, Large)

finished measurements
13½–16 (15½–18, 17½–20, 19½–22)" (34.5–40.5 [39.5–45.5, 44.5–51, 49.5–56]cm) maximum stretched circumference

gauge
16 stitches and 24 rows = 4" (10cm) in stockinette stitch

materials
50 (62, 76, 92) yd (45.5 [56.5, 69.5, 84]m) / 1 ball Lion Brand Yarn Vanna's Choice, 100% premium acrylic, 3½ oz (100g), 170 yd (156m), in desired color **(4)**

US size 8 (5mm) 16" (40.5cm) circular needle, or size needed to obtain gauge

Set of 5 US size 8 (5mm) double-pointed needles, or size needed to obtain gauge

Stitch marker

Blunt-end yarn needle

INSTRUCTIONS

With circular needle, knit cast on 54 (60, 66, 72) stitches. Do not join.

Note: Knit cast-on instructions are given on page 20.

Purl 1 row.

Place marker and join to work in the round, being careful not to twist stitches.

Work in garter stitch (knit 1 round, purl the next) for 4 rows.

Work in stockinette stitch (knit every round) for 14 (18, 22, 26) rounds.

SHAPE CROWN
Note: Switch to double-pointed needles when necessary.

Round 1: *K4, k2tog; repeat from * 9 (10, 11, 12) times—45 (50, 55, 60) stitches.

Rounds 2 and 3: Knit.

Round 4: *K3, k2tog; repeat from * 9 (10, 11, 12) times—36 (40, 44, 48) stitches.

Rounds 5 and 6: Knit.

Round 7: *K2, k2tog; repeat from * 9 (10, 11, 12) times—27 (30, 33, 36) stitches.

Round 8: Knit.

Round 9: K2tog 13 (15, 16, 18) times, k1 (0, 1, 0)—14 (15, 17, 18) stitches.

Round 10: K2tog 7 (7, 8, 9) times, k0 (1, 1, 0)—7 (8, 9, 9) stitches.

FINISH

Cut yarn, leaving a tail for closing. With blunt-end yarn needle, thread tail through the remaining stitches. Pull tightly and weave in end.

1ST EARFLAP

With double-pointed needle, right side facing, and starting at the front of the hat, pick up 10 (12, 14, 16) stitches along the cast-on edge.

Note: Decrease rounds are worked on the wrong side.

Row 1 (WS): *Ktbl; repeat from * to end of row.

Rows 2–4: Knit.

Row 5: K1, k2tog, knit to the last 3 stitches, k2tog, k1—2 stitches decreased.

Row 6: Knit.

Repeat the last 2 rows 2 (3, 4, 5) more times—4 stitches.

Last row: K1, k2tog, k1—3 stitches.

Work 3-stitch I-cord (page 150) until it measures approximately 9 (9, 10, 10)" (23 [23, 25.5, 25.5]cm).

Cut yarn. Weave in end.

2ND EARFLAP

With double-pointed needle, right side facing, and starting at the 17th (19th, 20th, 21st) stitch to the left of the 1st Earflap, pick up 10 (12, 14, 16) stitches on the cast-on edge.

Work as for 1st Earflap.

fingerless handsies

I have gifted tons of paw booties to babies in their first year of life and found that their older siblings were wearing them, too—not on their feet, but *on their hands*, growling ferociously or barking and fetching on all fours. With that in mind, I designed these fingerless mitts so that older children could have paws, too. You can make them, to complete an ensemble, for the Bear, Panda, Cat, and any other animal that has paws.

Very young children get frustrated if they don't have the dexterity to get their fingers into the openings by themselves, so I designed a simplified option for each size. Beware that once older children are introduced to the more complicated option, they will not let you compromise!

sizes
Small (Medium, Large)

finished measurements
6 (7, 8)" (15 [18, 20.5]cm) in circumference

gauge
16 stitches and 24 rows = 4" (10cm) in stockinette stitch

materials
29 (46, 66) yd (26.5 [42, 60.5]m) / 1 ball Lion Brand Yarn Vanna's Choice, 100% premium acrylic, 3½ oz (100g), 170 yd (156m), in desired color 4

Set of 5 US size 8 (5mm) double-pointed needles, or size needed to obtain gauge

Stitch marker

Stitch holder or large safety pin

Blunt-end yarn needle

INSTRUCTIONS

Knit cast on 20 (24, 28) stitches onto a double-pointed needle.

Join to work in the round on 2 needles, distributing evenly on first round—10 (12, 14) stitches on each needle.

Round 1: *K1, p1; repeat from * to end of round.

Repeat Round 1 to work in k1, p1 rib for 7 (8, 9) more rounds.

Knit 5 (7, 9) rounds.

> **»** Adorable Danika received her first pair of fingerless handsies when she was six years old and came to visit us with her nana. She put them on right away and kept them on while she had her snacks. Much later, coloring at the end of the kitchen island, she said, "I have to go potty. Will you help me, Nana?"
>
> "What?" said Nana with surprise. "Since when do you need me to help you go potty?"
>
> Danika put down her crayon and, holding up both hands with paw pads showing, said with exaggerated exasperation, "But Nana, I don't want to get these wet!" She wore that first pair all day, every day, everywhere she went, until she wore them out, in just a few short weeks.

THUMB GUSSET

Round 1: K9 (11, 13) to last stitch on front needle, M1, k1; k1, M1, knit to end of round—22 (26, 30) stitches.

Rounds 2, 4, and 6: Knit.

Round 3: K9 (11, 13) to last 2 stitches on front needle, M1, k2; k2, M1, knit to end of round—24 (28, 32) stitches.

Round 5: K9 (11, 13) to last 3 stitches on front needle, M1, k3; k3, M1, knit to end of round—26 (30, 34) stitches.

Sizes Medium (Large) only

Round 7: K11 (13) to last 4 stitches on front needle, M1, k4; k4, M1, knit to end of round—32 (36) stitches.

Round 8: Knit.

Size Large only

Round 9: K13 to last 5 stitches on front needle, M1, k5; k5, M1, knit to end of round—38 stitches.

Round 10: Knit.

All sizes

Next round: K10 (12, 14), slip 6 (8, 10) stitches onto a holder or large safety pin, knit to end of round—20 (24, 28) stitches remain. The held stitches will later be worked for the thumb. Divide the remaining stitches evenly over the 2 needles.

Note: For the simplified handsie without individual finger openings (opposite, right), simply knit 3 (6, 9) rows, then bind off all 20 (24, 28) stitches purlwise. Continue to Thumb instructions.

MAIN GLOVE

Knit 2 (5, 8) rounds.

Next round: *K3 (4, 5), M1, k4, M1, k3 (4, 5); repeat from * for back needle—24 (28, 32) stitches.

Next round: Knit.

PINKIE

Sizes Small (Medium) only

Step 1: Bind off 3 stitches purlwise on front needle. Turn work.

Step 2: Slip the leftmost 3 (4) stitches from the back needle onto the 4th, previously unused needle. This will become your back needle for this finger.

Step 3: Bind off the 3 (4) stitches on new back needle purlwise—18 (21) hand stitches remain unworked.

Size Large only

Step 1: K4.

Step 2: Slip the leftmost 4 stitches from the back needle onto the 4th, previously unused needle. This will become your back needle for this finger.

Step 3: K4 on back needle.

Step 4: Bind off the 8 Pinkie stitches purlwise—24 hand stitches remain unworked.

All sizes

Cut yarn 48 (72, 96)" (122 [183, 244] cm) long, stitch down the side of finger opening to the base, and sew a few stitches across the gap (see Long Ending Tails, page 22). Use tail to continue knitting.

POINTER FINGER

Step 1: Working in the round, knit the 6 (7, 8) remaining stitches 0 (1, 2) times.

Step 2: Bind off all Pointer Finger stitches purlwise.

Step 3: Close finger as for Pinkie.

Step 4: Weave in end.

THUMB

Remount 6 (8, 10) thumb stitches, distributing them evenly on 2 needles.

Rejoining yarn at top of thumb opening, k6 (8, 10), then pick up and knit 2 stitches at top of thumb opening—8 (10, 12) stitches.

Knit 0 (1, 2) rounds.

Bind off all stitches purlwise.

Cut yarn, leaving an 8" (20.5cm) tail. Thread through remaining stitch and close the opening with 1 or 2 stitches.

If the top of the thumb shows any gaps, fill in with a few stitches. Weave in end.

FINISHING

Cut paw pads (page 154) from felt and hot-glue them to the palms of handsies. Make sure you have opposing thumbs on the paw-pad sides!

RING FINGER

Step 1: K3 (4, 4).

Step 2: Slip the leftmost 3 (3, 4) stitches from the back needle onto the 4th needle as before and knit them.

Step 3: With right side facing, knit 0 (1, 2) rounds over these 2 needles—6 (7, 8) stitches.

Step 4: Bind off 6 (7, 8) Ring Finger stitches purlwise.

Step 5: Close finger as for Pinkie—12 (14, 16) hand stitches remain unworked.

MIDDLE FINGER

Step 1: K3 (3, 4).

Step 2: Slip the leftmost 3 (4, 4) stitches from the back needle onto the 4th needle and knit them as before.

Step 3: With the right side facing, knit 0 (1, 2) rounds over these 2 needles.

Step 4: Bind off 6 (7, 8) Middle Finger stitches purlwise.

Step 5: Close finger as for Pinkie—6 (7, 8) hand stitches remain unworked.

FOREST FAVORITES

>>>

bear
—
beaver
—
fox
—
owl
—
rabbit
—
toad

bear

The Bear works up so fast and easy. The only hard part is deciding what kind of bear to make—a teddy bear? A black bear? A polar bear? The matching booties are very simple to make because there are no toes to work up; however, if you want a more ferocious-looking bear, consider using the booties pattern shown with the Panda (page 104).

sizes
Newborn (Small, Medium, Large)

finished measurements
13½–16 (15½–18, 17½–20, 19½–22)" (34.5–40.5 [39.5–45.5, 44.5–51, 49.5–56]cm) maximum stretched circumference

gauge
16 stitches and 24 rows = 4" (10cm) in stockinette stitch

materials
For hat: 54 (66, 81, 95) yd (49.5 [60.5, 74, 87]m) / 1 ball Lion Brand Yarn Vanna's Choice, 100% premium acrylic, 3½ oz (100g), 170 yd (156m), in Honey, Black, or White (A), and 7, (7, 9, 9) yd (6.4 [6.5, 8, 8]m) in Chocolate, Honey, or White (B) (4)

For hat and booties set: 88 (117, 152, —) yd (80.5 [107, 139, —]m) / 1 ball Lion Brand Yarn Vanna's Choice, 100% premium acrylic, 3½ oz (100g), 170 yd (156m), in Honey, Black, or White (A), and 7, (7, 9, —) yd (6.4 [6.4, 8.2, —]m) in Chocolate, Honey, or White (B) (4)

US size 8 (5mm) 16" (40.5cm) circular needle, or size needed to obtain gauge

Set of 5 US size 8 (5mm) double-pointed needles, or size needed to obtain gauge

Stitch marker

Blunt-end yarn needle

Size F-5 (3.75mm) or G-6 (4mm) crochet hook

Styrofoam ball, 2 (2, 2½, 2½)" (5, [5, 6.5, 6.5]cm) in diameter

Serrated knife

Scrap of black yarn for mouth

Black plastic nose with post, 18 (18, 21, 21)mm

Side-cutting needle-nosed pliers

High-temperature (60-watt) hot-glue gun and glue sticks

Round glass bowl vase (see page 19)

Pair of doll eyes, 12 (12, 15, 15)mm

Black or brown felt for paw pads on booties and/or handsies (see Felt Templates, page 154)

BEAR HAT

With A, knit a Rolled-Brim Hat (page 28) or Earflap Hat (page 30).

(page 28) ... (page 30).

EARS

Lay the finished hat flat. With a crochet hook and starting at the 6th (7th, 8th, 9th) stitch from the center of the top of the hat, pick up 8 (8, 10, 10) stitches along the top edge of the hat. Transfer stitches to a double-pointed needle. Turn hat over to the back side. With a crochet hook, pick up 8 (8, 10, 10) stitches directly behind the stitches on the double-pointed needle—16 (16, 20, 20) stitches total.

Note: You will be working the ears on 2 needles, in the round, knitting the back stitches off the crochet hook on the 1st round (see Picking Up Stitches for Ears, page 21).

Round 1: *Ktbl; repeat to end of round.

Round 2: *K1, M1, knit to last stitch on needle, M1, k1; repeat from * for back needle—20 (20, 24, 24) stitches; 10 (10, 12, 12) stitches each needle.

Round 3: Knit.

Round 4: *K1, k2tog, knit to last 3 stitches on needle, k2tog, k1; repeat from * for back needle—16 (16, 20, 20) stitches; 8 (8, 10, 10) stitches each needle.

Round 5: Knit.

Repeat rounds 4 and 5 once (once, twice, twice) more—12 stitches; 6 stitches each needle.

Last round: *K1, k2tog, k2tog, k1; repeat from * for back needle—8 stitches; 4 stitches on each needle.

Cut yarn, leaving a tail for sewing, and thread through remaining 8 stitches with a blunt-end needle. With the tail, sew a few stitches across the opening, so the finished edge is straight.

SNOUT

With B, using double-pointed needles, and leaving a 12" (30.5cm) tail for finishing, knit cast on 30 (30, 33, 33) stitches.

Knit 1 row.

Join to work in the round as follows: K6 (6, 7, 7) on 1st needle, k18 on 2nd needle, k6 (6, 8, 8) on 3rd needle. Using 3rd needle, k6 (6, 7, 7) from 1st needle—18 stitches on the front needle; 12 (12, 15, 15) stitches on the back needle.

Knit 3 (3, 5, 5) rounds.

Round 1: *K1, k2tog; repeat from * to end of round—20 (20, 22, 22)

> **»** My twelve-year-old Knit Wizard, Lamara, who is fearless about modifying my patterns (as I hope you will be, too), made a pink Care Bear from this pattern. We simply gave him a heart-shaped felt nose, felt ear inserts, and embroidered eyebrows.

stitches; 12 stitches on front needle and 8 (8, 10, 10) stitches on back needle.

Round 2: Knit.

Round 3: *K2tog; repeat from * to end of round—10 (10, 11, 11) stitches.

Cut yarn and thread through remaining 10 (10, 11, 11) stitches with blunt-end needle. Weave in end.

Cut the Styrofoam ball in half with a serrated knife.

Enclose Styrofoam into knit Snout, following the directions for Simple Snouts (page 23).

FINISH BEAR HAT

Sew the Bear's mouth, following the photo, beginning and ending the line of stitches where the plastic nose will be placed (see Stitching a Mouth, page 22).

With a double-pointed needle, make a hole in the center of the Snout to fit the post on the back of the plastic nose. Hot-glue the nose into and around the hole, making sure that the hot glue bonds the yarn to the back of the nose (see Plastic Animal Noses, page 18).

Stretch the hat over a glass vase and hot-glue the Snout in place. Snip the posts off the eyes and hot-glue them in place.

BEAR BOOTIES (make 2)

Knit cast on 16 (20, 24) stitches onto a double-pointed needle.

Join to work in the round as follows: K4 (5, 6) on 1st needle, k8 (10, 12) on 2nd needle, k4 (5, 6) stitches on 3rd needle. Using 3rd needle, k4 (5, 6) from 1st needle—8 (10, 12) stitches on each needle.

Knit 14 (19, 24) rounds.

HEEL FLAP

Note: The heel flap is worked back and forth in rows over the back needle.

Turn work.

Beginning with a wrong-side row, work 7 rows in stockinette stitch (k on RS, p on WS).

Row 8 (RS): Sl 1 knitwise, k3 (5, 7), skp. Turn work.

Row 9 (WS): Sl 1 purlwise, p1 (3, 5), p2tog. Turn work.

Row 10: Sl 1 knitwise, k1 (3, 5), skp. Turn work.

Row 11: Sl 1 purlwise, p1 (3, 5), p2tog. Turn work.

Row 12: Sl 1 knitwise, k1 (3, 5), skp. Turn work—3 (5, 7) stitches.

Row 13: Purl.

Row 14: Knit.

GUSSETS

With back needle, pick up 5 stitches from the left side of the heel flap (1 stitch in each knot along the edge).

K8 (10, 12) stitches over the front needle.

With a 3rd needle, pick up 6 stitches along the other side of the heel flap, then k8 (10, 12) from back needle onto this new needle—22 (26, 30) stitches; 8 (10, 12) stitches on the front needle and 14 (16, 18) stitches on the back needle.

Round 1: Knit.

Round 2: Knit across front needle; k1, k2tog, knit to last 3 stitches on back needle, k2tog, k1—2 stitches decreased.

Repeat the last 2 rounds twice more—16 (20, 24) stitches; 8 (10, 12) stitches on each needle.

Knit 1 (4, 7) rounds.

SHAPE FOOT

Round 1: *K4 (5, 6), M1, k4 (5, 6); repeat from * for back needle—18 (22, 26) stitches; 9 (11, 13) stitches on each needle.

Round 2: Knit.

Round 3: *K4 (5, 6), M1, k5 (6, 7); repeat from * for needle—20 (24, 28) stitches; 10 (12, 14) stitches on each needle.

Round 4: Knit.

Round 5: *K5 (6, 7), M1, k5 (6, 7); repeat from * for back needle—22 (26, 30) stitches; 11 (13, 15) stitches on each needle.

Round 6: Knit.

Round 7: *K5 (6, 7), M1, k6 (7, 8); repeat from * for back needle—24 (28, 32) stitches; 12 (14, 16) stitches on each needle.

Round 8: Knit.

Round 9: *K1, k2tog, knit to last 3 stitches, k2tog, k1; repeat from * for back needle—4 stitches decreased.

Repeat the last round 2 (3, 4) more times—12 stitches; 6 stitches each needle.

Cut yarn and thread through the remaining 12 stitches with blunt-end needle. With tail, sew a few stitches across the opening, creating a straight finished edge.

Weave in ends.

FINISH BEAR BOOTIES

Cut a pair of paw pads (page 154) from felt and hot-glue to the bottom of Bear Booties.

NEWBORN BEAR HANDSIES
(make 2)

Knit cast on 16 stitches onto a double-pointed needle and join in the round as for Bear Booties.

Knit 10 rounds.

Shape foot and add paw pads as for Bear Booties.

beaver

This hat makes everyone laugh out loud. There's just something about those teeth! Unlike the Bear's simple snout (see page 23), it takes two components to make the Beaver's face: a nose triangle and chubby cheeks. When I am making a gift for a newborn, I always make handsies instead of booties. Handsies work up in much less time than booties because there's no heel or foot length to knit, but they still deliver 100 percent hilarity.

sizes
Newborn (Small, Medium, Large)

finished measurements
13½–16 (15½–18, 17½–20, 19½–22)" (34.5–40.5 [39.5–45.5, 44.5–51, 49.5–56]cm) maximum stretched circumference

gauge
16 stitches and 24 rows = 4" (10cm) in stockinette stitch

materials
For hat: 47 (59, 71, 85) yd (43 [54, 65, 78]m) / 1 ball Lion Brand Yarn Vanna's Choice, 100% premium acrylic, 3½ oz (100g), 170 yd (156m), in Toffee (4)

For hat and booties set: 95 (123, 161, —) yd (87 [112.5, 147, —]m) / 1 ball Lion Brand Yarn Vanna's Choice, 100% premium acrylic, 3½ oz (100g), 170 yd (156m), in Toffee (4)

US size 8 (5mm) 16" (40.5cm) circular needle, or size needed to obtain gauge

Set of 5 US size 8 (5mm) double-pointed needles, or size needed to obtain gauge

Stitch marker

Blunt-end yarn needle

Size F-5 (3.75mm) or G-6 (4mm) crochet hook

Styrofoam ball, 1½ (1½, 2, 2)" (3.8 [3.8, 5, 5]cm) in diameter

Serrated knife

1½ yd (1.4m) white yarn for teeth

High-temperature (60-watt) hot-glue gun and glue sticks

Black plastic nose with post, 18 (18, 21, 21)mm

Round glass bowl vase (see page 19)

Pair of solid black eyes, 9 (9, 12, 12)mm

Side-cutting needle-nosed pliers

Scrap of white felt for eyes

BEAVER HAT

Knit a Rolled-Brim Hat (page 28) or Earflap Hat (page 30).

EARS (make 2)

Lay the finished hat flat. With a crochet hook and starting at the 6th (7th, 8th, 9th) stitch from the center of the top of the hat, pick up 4 (4, 5, 5) stitches along the top edge of the hat. Transfer stitches to a double-pointed needle. Turn hat over to the back side. With a crochet hook, pick up 4 (4, 5, 5) stitches directly behind the stitches on the double-pointed needle—8 (8, 10, 10) stitches total.

Note: You will be working the ears on 2 needles, in the round, knitting the back stitches off the crochet hook on the 1st round (see Picking Up Stitches for Ears, page 21).

Round 1: *Ktbl; repeat to end of round.

Round 2: Knit.

Round 3: *K1, **M1, k1; repeat from ** to end of needle; repeat from * for back needle—14 (14, 18, 18) stitches; 7 (7, 9, 9) stitches on each needle.

Round 4: Knit.

Round 5: *K1, k2tog, knit to the last 3 stitches on needle, k2tog, k1; repeat from * for back needle –4 stitches decreased.

Round 6: Knit.

Sizes Medium and Large only
Repeat Rounds 5 and 6 once more—10 stitches; 5 stitches on each needle.

All sizes
Cut yarn and thread through the remaining 3 (3, 5, 5) stitches with blunt-end needle. Weave in ends.

CHEEKS

With one double-pointed needle and leaving a 12" (30.5cm) tail for sewing, cast on 21 (21, 27, 27) stitches.

Beginning with a right-side row, work 8 (8, 12, 12) rows in stockinette stitch (knit on RS, purl on WS).

Decrease row (RS): *K1, k2tog; repeat from * to end of row—14 (14, 18, 18) stitches.

Beginning with a wrong-side row, work 3 rows in stockinette stitch.

To bind off, pass all of the stitches over the 1st stitch until 1 stitch remains. Cut yarn, leaving a 6" (15cm) tail for finishing, and thread through the remaining stitch on a blunt-end yarn needle.

FINISH CHEEKS

Cut 2 pieces from the 1½ (1½, 2, 2)" (3.8 [3.8, 5, 5]cm) Styrofoam ball, each ⅛" (3mm) shy of center. Discard the ¼" (6mm) leftover center disk.

Enclose Styrofoam into knit Cheeks, following the directions for Cheeks (page 24).

NOSE TRIANGLE

With double-pointed needles and leaving a 9" (23cm) tail for sewing, knit cast on 20 (20, 24, 24) stitches.

Join to work in the round as follows: K5 (5, 6, 6) on 1st needle, k10 (10, 12, 12) on 2nd needle, k5 (5, 6, 6) on 3rd needle. Using 3rd needle, k5 (5, 6, 6) from 1st needle—10 (10, 12, 12) stitches on each needle.

Round 1: Knit.

Round 2: *K1, k2tog, k to last 3 stitches on needle, k2tog, k1; repeat from * for back needle—4 stitches decreased.

Repeat the last round 2 (2, 3, 3) more times—8 stitches; 4 stitches on each needle.

Next round: * K1, k2tog, k1; repeat from * once—6 stitches; 3 stitches on each needle.

Cut yarn and thread through the remaining 6 stitches with blunt-end needle. Weave in end, leaving cast-on tail for finishing.

Follow directions for finishing Nose Triangles (page 24).

TEETH (make 2)

With the scrap of white yarn, cast on 3 (3, 4, 4) stitches onto a double-pointed needle.

Work these 3 (3, 4, 4) stitches as I-cord (page 150) for 9 (9, 12, 12) rows.

Cut yarn. Thread through all stitches using blunt-end needle and weave in ends.

FINISH BEAVER HAT

Hot-glue the black plastic nose into the Cheeks (see Plastic Animal Noses, page 18). Hot-glue the knit Nose Triangle behind the Cheeks, making sure that the triangle bulges in the center. Hot-glue the Teeth behind the Cheeks.

Stretch the hat over a glass vase and hot-glue the face in place. Cut eye pieces out of white felt. Snip the post off the eyes and glue them onto white felt. Glue the felt-backed eyes in place.

BEAVER BOOTIES (make 2)

Knit cast on 16 (20, 24) stitches onto a double-pointed needle.

Join to work in the round as follows: K4 (5, 6) on 1st needle, k8 (10, 12) on 2nd needle, k4 (5, 6) on 3rd needle. Using 3rd needle, k4 (5, 6) from 1st needle—8 (10, 12) stitches on each needle.

Knit 14 (19, 24) rounds.

HEEL FLAP

Note: The heel flap is worked back and forth in rows over the back needle.

Turn work.

Beginning with a wrong-side row, work 7 rows in stockinette stitch (k on RS, p on WS).

Row 8 (RS): Sl 1 knitwise, k3 (5, 7), skp. Turn work.

Row 9 (WS): Sl 1 purlwise, p1 (3, 5), p2tog. Turn work.

Row 10: Sl 1 knitwise, k1 (3, 5), skp. Turn work.

Row 11: Sl 1 purlwise, p1 (3, 5), p2tog. Turn work.

Row 12: Sl 1 knitwise, k1 (3, 5), skp. Turn work—3 (5, 7) stitches.

Row 13: Purl.

Row 14: Knit.

GUSSETS

With back needle, k3 (5, 7), and pick up 5 stitches from the left side of the heel flap (1 stitch in each knot along the top edge).

K8 (10, 12) stitches over the front needle.

With a 3rd needle, pick up 6 stitches along the other side of the heel flap, then k8 (10, 12) from the back needle onto this new needle—22 (26, 30) stitches; 8 (10, 12) stitches on front needle and 14 (16, 18) stitches on back needle.

Round 1: Knit.

Round 2: Knit across front needle; k1, k2tog, knit to last 3 stitches on back needle, k2tog, k1—2 stitches decreased.

Repeat the last 2 rounds twice more—16 (20, 24) stitches; 8 (10, 12) stitches on each needle.

Knit 9 (14, 17) rounds.

Size Newborn only
Next round: *K2, M1, k4, M1, k2; repeat from * for back needle—20 stitches; 10 stitches on each needle.

Size Medium only
Next round: *K2, k2tog, k2, ssk, k2; repeat from * for back needle—20 stitches; 10 stitches on each needle.

All sizes
Next round: K18, leaving 2 stitches unworked on back needle.

MAKE TOES

Note: Outer toes are worked first.

Toe 1 (far right)
With a 3rd needle, k2tog (the remaining 2 unworked stitches on back needle), then k2tog from front needle.

Work these 2 stitches as I-cord (page 150) for 2 rounds.

Cut yarn, leaving a 48" (122cm) long tail, and thread through the 2 stitches using a blunt-end needle. Pull tightly and thread long tail through to the bottom of toe and sew a few stitches across the gap (see Long Ending Tails, page 22). Use tail for the remaining toes.

Toe 2 (far left)
K6, leaving 2 stitches unworked on front needle.

With a 3rd needle, k2tog (the remaining 2 unworked stitches on front needle), then k2tog from back needle.

Work these 2 stitches as I-cord for 2 rounds.

Thread tail through the 2 stitches using a blunt-end needle. Pull tightly and thread long tail through to the bottom of toe, and sew a few stitches across the gap.

Toe 3 (inner right)
K4, leaving 2 stitches unworked on back needle.

With a 3rd needle, k2tog (the remaining 2 unworked stitches on back needle), then k2tog from front needle.

Work these 2 stitches as I-cord for 2 rounds.

Thread tail through the 2 stitches using a blunt-end needle. Pull tightly and thread tail through to the bottom of toe and sew a few stitches across the gap

Toe 4 (inner left)
K2, leaving 2 stitches unworked on front needle.

With a 3rd needle, finish as for Toe 2.

Toe 5 (middle)
K2—no stitches remain on back needle.

With a 3rd needle, k2tog twice.

Work these 2 stitches as I-cord for 2 rounds.

Thread tail through the 2 stitches using a blunt-end needle. Pull tightly and weave in end.

NEWBORN BEAVER HANDSIES (make 2)
Knit cast on 16 stitches onto double-pointed needles and join in the round as for Beaver Booties.

Knit 18 rounds.

Next round: *K2, M1, k4, M1, k2; repeat from * for back needle—10 stitches each needle.

Next round: K18, leaving 2 stitches unworked on back needle.

Make toes as for Beaver Booties.

fox

Lion Brand created a new line for Jo-Ann Fabric and Craft Store named Heartland that's easy to substitute for Vanna's Choice because the yarns are the exact same weight. For this Gramminal, I chose a yummy color called Yosemite that is a rusty shade with thin strands of red running through it, giving the Fox an added dimension of realism. Heartland comes in a large skein, which gives you enough to make a set for the new baby as well as for big brother or sister.

sizes
Newborn (Small, Medium, Large)

finished measurements
13½–16 (15½–18, 17½–20, 19½–22)" (34.5–40.5 [39.5–45.5, 44.5–51, 49.5–56]cm) maximum stretched circumference

gauge
16 stitches and 24 rows = 4" (10cm) in stockinette stitch

materials
For hat: 59 (72, 89, 105) yd (54 [66, 81.5, 96]m) / 1 skein Lion Brand Yarn Heartland, 100% premium acrylic, 5 oz (142g), 251 yd (230m), in Yosemite (A) (4) ; 8 (8, 11, 11) yd (7.5 [7.5, 10, 10]m) / 1 ball Lion Brand Yarn Vanna's Choice, 100% premium acrylic, 3½ oz (100g), 170 yd (156m), in White (B) (4)

For hat and booties set: 93, (123, 157, —) yd (85 [112.5, 143.5, —]m) / 1 skein Lion Brand Yarn Heartland, 100% premium acrylic, 5 oz (142g), 251 yd (230m), in Yosemite (A) (4) ; 8 (8, 11, —) yd (7.5 [7.5, 10, —]m) / 1 ball Lion Brand Yarn Vanna's Choice, 100% premium acrylic, 3½ oz (100g), 170 yd (156m), in White (B) (4)

US size 8 (5mm) 16" (40.5cm) circular needle, or size needed to obtain gauge

Set of 5 US size 8 (5mm) double-pointed needles, or size needed to obtain gauge

Stitch marker

Blunt-end yarn needle

Size F-5 (3.75mm) or G-6 (4mm) crochet hook

Styrofoam ball, 1 (1, 1½, 1½)" (2.5 [2.5, 3.8, 3.8]cm) in diameter

Serrated knife

High-temperature (60-watt) hot-glue gun and glue sticks

- Black plastic nose with post, 18 (18, 21, 21)mm
- Black felt for eyes and tongue, and for paw pads on booties and/or handsies
- Polyester fiberfill
- Scrap of black and mustard-colored felt for eyes
- Pair of animal eyes, 18mm
- Side-cutting needle-nosed pliers
- Round glass bowl vase (see page 19)

FOX HAT

With A, knit a Rolled-Brim Hat (page 28) or Earflap Hat (page 30).

EARS (make 2)

Lay the finished hat flat. With a crochet hook and starting at the 4th (5th, 6th, 7th) stitch from the center of the top of the hat, pick up 12 (14, 16, 18) stitches along the top edge of the hat. Transfer stitches to a double-pointed needle. Turn hat over to the back side. With a crochet hook, pick up 12 (14, 16, 18) stitches directly behind the stitches on the double-pointed needle—24 (28, 32, 36) stitches total.

Note: You will be working the ears on 2 needles, in the round, knitting the back stitches off the crochet hook on the 1st round (see Picking Up Stitches for Ears, page 21).

Round 1: *Ktbl; repeat to end of round.

Round 2: K1, M1, knit to the last 2 stitches on front needle, k2tog; k2tog, knit to the last stitch on back needle, M1, k1.

Round 3: Knit to the last 2 stitches on front needle, k2tog; k2tog, knit to the end of round on back needle—2 stitches decreased.

Round 4: Repeat Round 3—20 (24, 28, 32) stitches; 10 (12, 14, 16) stitches on each needle.

Round 5: Repeat Round 2.

Repeat Round 3 one (three, five, seven) times—18 stitches; 9 stitches on each needle.

Cut yarn, leaving a 4" (10cm) tail. Change to B.

Next round: With B, *k2tog, k5, k2tog; repeat from * for back needle—14 stitches; 7 stitches on each needle.

Next round: Knit to last 2 stitches on front needle, k2tog; k2tog, knit to end of round on back needle—2 stitches decreased.

Repeat the last round 4 more times—4 stitches; 2 stitches on each needle.

Cut yarn and thread through the remaining 4 stitches with blunt-end needle. Weave in ends.

CHEEKS

With B, u double-pointed needle, and leaving a 12" (30.5cm) tail for sewing, knit cast on 18 (18, 21, 21) stitches.

Beginning with a right-side row, work 4 (4, 8, 8) rows flat in stockinette stitch (knit on RS, purl on WS).

Decrease row (RS): *K1, k2tog; repeat from * to the end—12 (12, 14, 14) stitches.

Beginning with a wrong-side row, work 3 rows in stockinette stitch.

To bind off, pass all of the stitches over the 1st stitch until 1 stitch remains. Cut yarn, leaving a 6" (15cm) tail for finishing and thread through the remaining stitch with a blunt-end needle.

FINISH CHEEKS

Sizes Newborn and Small only
Cut 1" (2.5cm) Styrofoam ball in half to create 2 cheeks.

Sizes Medium and Large only
Cut 2 pieces from the 1½" (3.8cm) Styrofoam ball, each ⅛" (3mm) shy of center. Discard the ¼" (6mm) leftover center disk.

All sizes
Enclose Styrofoam into knit Cheeks, following the directions for Cheeks (page 24).

JAW

With B, using double-pointed needles, and leaving a 9" (23cm) tail for sewing, knit cast on 12 stitches.

Join to work in the round as follows: K3 on 1st needle, k6 on 2nd needle, k3 on 3rd needle

Using 3rd needle, k3 from 1st needle—6 stitches on each needle.

Knit 2 rounds.

Next round: *K1, k2tog; repeat from * to end of round—8 stitches; 4 on each needle.

Next round: *K2tog; repeat from * to end of round—4 stitches; 2 on each needle.

Cut yarn and thread through the remaining 4 stitches with blunt-end needle. Weave in end.

Follow directions for finishing Jaws (page 24).

LONG SNOUT

With A, using double-pointed needles, and leaving a 12" (30.5cm) tail for sewing, knit cast on 30 (30, 42, 42) stitches.

Knit 1 row.

Join to work in the round as follows: K6 (6, 12, 12) on 1st needle, k18 on 2nd needle, k6 (6, 12, 12) on 3rd needle. Using 3rd needle, k6 (6, 9, 9) from 1st needle—18 stitches on front needle and 12 (12, 24, 24) stitches on back needle.

Round 1: Knit.

Round 2: *K4, k2tog; repeat from * to end of round—25 (25, 35, 35) stitches; 15 stitches on front needle and 10 (10, 20, 20) stitches on back needle.

Round 3: Knit.

Round 4: *K3, k2tog; repeat from * to end of round—20 (20, 28, 28) stitches; 12 stitches on front needle and 8 (8, 16, 16) stitches on back needle.

Round 5: Knit.

Round 6: *K2, k2tog; repeat from * to end of round—15 (15, 21, 21) stitches; 9 stitches on front needle and 6 (6, 12, 12) stitches on back needle.

Round 7: Knit.

Round 8: Purl.

Round 9: Knit.

Round 10: *K1, k2tog; repeat from * to end of round—10 (10, 14, 14) stitches; 6 stitches on front needle and 4 (4, 8, 8) stitches on back needle.

Round 11: *K2tog; repeat from * to end of round—3 stitches on front needle and 2 (2, 4, 4) stitches on back needle. Cut yarn and thread through the remaining 5 (5, 7, 7) stitches with blunt-end needle. Weave in end.

With cast-on tail, finish following directions for Long Snouts (page 25).

FINISH FOX HAT

Hot-glue the black plastic nose between the Cheeks. Cut a teardrop shape of black felt for the tongue and hot-glue it into the center of the Jaw.

Stuff the Snout and attach the Cheeks and Jaw following directions for Long Snouts (page 25).

Note: If the Snout needs a little more stuffing after it has been attached to the hat, add more fiberfill by rolling small pieces into balls and poking them through from the outside with the tip of a double-pointed needle.

Cut 2 eye shapes from black felt and 2 slightly smaller eye shapes from yellow felt. Hot-glue the yellow felt to the black felt. Snip the posts off the eyes and hot-glue in place on the yellow felt. Stretch the hat over a glass vase and hot-glue the felt eye shapes in place.

FOX BOOTIES (make 2)

With A, follow pattern instructions for Bear Booties (page 41).

NEWBORN FOX HANDSIES (make 2)

With A, follow pattern instructions for Newborn Bear Handsies (page 42).

owl

There is nothing frivolous about this owl, who is smart and serious and who commands respect. To add to his richness, I use a heather yarn that gives this wise bird an even-more-realistic quality. Simple shapes cut from acrylic felt are used to create the eyes. Try experimenting with felt to create eyes with unique expressions for other animal hats, too.

sizes

Newborn (Small, Medium, Large)

finished measurements

13½–16 (15½–18, 17½–20, 19½–22)" (34.5–40.5 [39.5–45.5, 44.5–51, 49.5–56]cm) maximum stretched circumference

gauge

16 stitches and 24 rows = 4" (10cm) in stockinette stitch

materials

For hat: 56 (70, 86, 103) yd (51 [64, 78.5, 94]m) / 1 ball Lion Brand Yarn Vanna's Choice, 100% premium acrylic, 3 oz (85g), 145 yd (133m), in Oatmeal or Barley (A), and 8 (10, 12, 15) yd (7.5 [9, 11, 14]m) in Mustard (B) **④**

For hat and booties set: 56 (70, 86, —) yd (51 [64, 78.5, —]m) / 1 ball Lion Brand Yarn Vanna's Choice, 100% premium acrylic, 3 oz (85g), 145 yd (133m), in Oatmeal or Barley (A), and 44 (62, 84, —) yd (40 [56.5, 77, —]m) in Mustard (B) **④**

US size 8 (5mm) 16" (40.5cm) circular needle, or size needed to obtain gauge

Set of 5 US size 8 (5mm) double-pointed needles, or size needed to obtain gauge

Stitch marker

Blunt-end yarn needle

High-temperature (60-watt) hot-glue gun and glue sticks

Pair of black wiggle eyes, 25mm

Scrap of white felt for the eyes

Pair of yellow wiggle eyes, 7mm

Round glass bowl vase (see page 19)

OWL HAT

With A, knit a Rolled-Brim Hat (page 28) or Earflap Hat (page 30).

CROWN TRIANGLE

With A and double-pointed needles, cast on 2 stitches.

Row 1: K1, kfb—3 stitches.

Row 2: K2, kfb—4 stitches.

Row 3: Knit to last stitch, kfb—1 stitch increased.

Repeat the last row 17 (21, 25, 29) times—22 (26, 30, 34) stitches.

Bind off all stitches and weave in end.

EARS (make 2)

With A and 2 double-pointed needles, and leaving a 12" (30.5cm) tail for finishing, knit cast on 2 stitches.

Row 1: Knit.

Row 2: Knit to last stitch, kfb—3 stitches.

Row 3: Kfb, knit to end—4 stitches.

Row 4: Knit to last stitch, kfb—5 stitches.

Sizes Medium and Large only

Row 5: Kfb, knit to end—6 stitches.

Row 6: Knit to last stitch, kfb—7 stitches.

All sizes

Bind off all stitches, leaving 12" (30.5cm) tail for sewing.

FINISH CROWN

Line up the Ears with the corners of the Crown Triangle along the bound-off edge. Using the outside tail, sew the edge of each Ear behind the Crown Triangle, up to the tip and down the other side, leaving both the bottom unsewn and the remaining tail for finishing.

Using the longest remaining tail and sewing across to the Ear, attach the Crown Triangle to the top of the hat, just in front of the center stitch. Sew across to the Ear. Sew the base of the Ear to the hat, propping up the corner of the Crown Triangle. Repeat on the other side.

Pull on the cast-on tail to slightly stretch the Crown Triangle, and sew the tip to the hat.

TOP BEAK

With B, using double-pointed needles, and leaving a 12" (30.5cm) tail for finishing, knit cast on 30 (34, 38, 42) stitches.

Join to work in the round as follows: K7 (8, 9, 10) on 1st needle, k16 (18, 20, 22) on 2nd needle, k7 (8, 9, 10) on 3rd needle. Using 3rd needle, k7 (8, 9, 10) from 1st needle—16 (18, 20, 22) stitches on front needle and 14 (16, 18, 20) stitches on back needle.

Round 1: *K1, k2tog, knit to last 3 stitches on needle, k2tog, k1; repeat

Next round: K2tog to end—3 stitches; 2 stitches on front needle and 1 stitch on back needle.

Cut yarn and thread through the remaining 3 stitches with blunt-end needle. Weave in end, leaving cast-on tail for finishing.

BOTTOM BEAK

With B, using double-pointed needles, and leaving a 12" (30.5cm) tail for finishing, knit cast on 18 (22, 26, 30) stitches.

Join to work in the round as follows: K4 (5, 6, 7) on 1st needle, k10 (12, 14, 16) on 2nd needle, k4 (5, 6, 7) on 3rd needle. Using 3rd needle, k4 (5, 6, 7) stitches from 1st needle—10 (12, 14, 16) stitches on front needle and 8 (10, 12, 14) stitches on back needle.

Decrease round: *K1, k2tog, knit to last 3 stitches on needle, k2tog, k1; repeat from * for back needle—4 stitches decreased.

Repeat decrease round 1 (2, 3, 4) more times—10 stitches; 6 stitches on front needle and 4 stitches on back needle.

Next round: *K1, k2tog twice; repeat from * once—6 stitches; 4 stitches on front needle and 2 stitches on back needle.

Next round: *K2tog; repeat from * to end of round—3 stitches; 2 stitches on front needle and 1 stitch on back needle.

from * for back needle—4 stitches decreased.

Round 2: Repeat Round 1—22 (26, 30, 34) stitches; 12 (14, 16, 18) stitches on front needle and 10 (12, 14, 16) stitches on back needle.

Round 3: Knit.

Repeat last 3 rounds 1 (2, 2, 3) more times—14 (10, 14, 10) stitches; 8 (6, 8, 6) stitches on front needle and 6 (4, 6, 4) stitches on back needle.

Repeat Round 1 one (zero, one, zero) more time(s)—10 stitches; 6 stitches on front needle and 4 stitches on back needle.

Next round: K1, k2tog twice, k1; k2tog twice—6 stitches; 4 stitches on front needle and 2 stitches on back needle.

Cut yarn and thread through the remaining 3 stitches with blunt-end needle. Weave in end, leaving cast-on tail for finishing.

FINISH BEAK

Sew the Top Beak following the directions for Beaks and Bills (page 25), pinching a prominent ridge *only* on the top side.

Sew the Bottom Beak in the same way as with the Top Beak, but pull the tail as tight as possible so that it closes up, like a roll-up bug, at the wide end.

Hot-glue the Bottom Beak into the Top Beak, which will hang over the edge slightly.

EYES

Using a 25mm wiggle eye as a guide, cut 2 circles out of white felt. Extract the plastic disks from each pair (black and yellow) of wiggle eyes. Hot-glue the black disk to the white felt, then hot-glue the yellow disk to the black disk.

FINISH OWL HAT

Stretch the hat over a glass vase. Pinch a ridge down the front of the Top Beak to find the center. Hot-glue only the Bottom Beak to the Hat, onto the tip of the Crown Triangle, and hold in place until it dries. Then glue the Top Beak, securing the pinch while holding it until it dries.

Glue each eye partially under the straight edge of the Crown Triangle and secure its placement by gluing the Crown Triangle to the eye.

OWL BOOTIES (make 2)

With B and using double-pointed needles, knit cast on 16 (20, 24) stitches.

Join to work in the round as follows: K4 (5, 6) on 1st needle, k8 (10, 12) on 2nd needle, k4 (5, 6) on 3rd needle. Using 3rd needle, k4 (5, 6) stitches from 1st needle—8 (10, 12) stitches on each needle.

Knit 14 (19, 24) rounds.

HEEL FLAP

Note: The heel flap is worked back and forth in rows over the back needle.

Turn work.

Beginning with a wrong-side row, work 7 rows in stockinette stitch (k on RS, p on WS).

Row 8 (RS): Sl 1 knitwise, k3 (5, 7), skp. Turn work.

Row 9 (WS): Sl 1 purlwise, p1 (3, 5), p2tog. Turn work.

Row 10: Sl 1 knitwise, k1 (3, 5), skp. Turn work.

Row 11: Sl 1 purlwise, p1 (3, 5), p2tog. Turn work.

Row 12: Sl 1 knitwise, k1 (3, 5), skp. Turn work.

Row 13: Purl.

Row 14: Knit.

GUSSETS

With back needle, k3 (5, 7), and pick up 5 stitches from the left side of the heel flap (1 stitch in each knot along the edge.)

K8 (10, 12) stitches over the front needle.

With 3rd needle, pick up 6 stitches along the other side of the heel flap, then k8 (10, 12) from back needle onto this new needle—22 (26, 30) stitches; 8 (10, 12) stitches on the front needle and 14 (16, 18) stitches on the back needle.

Round 1: Knit.

Round 2: Knit across front needle, k1, k2tog, knit to last 3 stitches on back needle, k2tog, k1—2 stitches decreased.

Repeat last 2 rounds twice more—16 (20, 24) stitches; 8 (10, 12) stitches on each needle.

Knit 11 (14, 18) rounds.

Size Small only
Next round: K2, k2tog, k2, ssk, k2; repeat from * for back needle—16 stitches; 8 stitches on each needle.

Size Medium only
Next round: K1, ssk, k2tog, k2, ssk, k2tog, k1; repeat from * for back needle—16 stitches; 8 stitches on each needle.

Toe 1 (right)

Slip the last 2 stitches on the back needle onto a 3rd needle and use this 3rd needle to knit the first 2 stitches from the front needle.

Work these 4 stitches as I-cord (page 150) for 4 rounds.

Cut yarn, leaving a 48" (122cm) long tail, and thread through the 4 stitches with blunt-end needle. Pull tightly, and thread long tail through to the bottom of the toe and sew a few stitches across the gap (see Long Ending Tails, page 22). Use tail for remaining toes—12 stitches remain unworked.

Toe 2 (left)

K2tog, ssk on front needle—2 stitches remaining.

Use a 3rd needle to knit last 2 stitches from front needle and to knit 2 stitches from back needle.

Work these 4 stitches on the 3rd needle as I-cord for 4 rounds.

Thread the long tail through all 4 stitches with blunt-end needle. Pull tightly, thread tail through the toe, and sew a few stitches across the gap—6 stitches remain unworked; 2 on front needle and 4 on back needle.

Toe 3 (middle)

*K2tog, ssk on back needle—4 stitches; 2 on front needle and 2 on back needle.

Work these 4 stitches as I-cord for 4 rounds. Thread the tail through all 4 stitches with blunt-end needle. Pull tightly, and thread tail through the toe. Check between toes to make sure there are no openings left unsewn. Weave in end.

NEWBORN OWL HANDSIES (make 2)

Knit cast on 16 stitches onto double-pointed needles and join in the round as for Owl Booties.

Knit 20 rounds.

Make toes as for Owl Booties.

rabbit

Expect lots of oohs and aahs when this little bunny hops out of your gift box. The Rabbit's ears are picked up differently than other Gramminals' in order to create a tubular base that can be stuffed with fiberfill. This technique creates absolutely adorable bent ears that can stand up on their own. The matching booties are an absolute riot, too!

sizes
Newborn (Small, Medium, Large)

finished measurements
13½–16 (15½–18, 17½–20, 19½–22)" (34.5–40.5 [39.5–45.5, 44.5–51, 49.5–56]cm) maximum stretched circumference

gauge
16 stitches and 24 rows = 4" (10cm) in stockinette stitch

materials
For hat: 75 (86, 115, 128) yd (68.5 [78.5, 105, 117]m) / 1 ball Lion Brand Yarn Vanna's Choice, 100% premium acrylic, 3½ oz (100g), 170 yd (156m), in White (4)

For hat and booties set: 109 (137, 185, —) yd (100 [125, 169, —]m) / 1 (1, 2, —) balls Lion Brand Yarn Vanna's Choice, 100% premium acrylic, 3½ oz (100g), 170 yd (156m), in White (4)

US size 8 (5mm) 16" (40.5cm) circular needle, or size needed to obtain gauge

Set of 5 US size 8 (5mm) double-pointed needles, or size needed to obtain gauge

Stitch marker

Blunt-end yarn needle

Size F-5 (3.75mm) or G-6 (4mm) crochet hook

Polyester fiberfill

Styrofoam ball, 1½ (1½, 2, 2)" (3.8 [3.8, 5, 5]cm) in diameter

Serrated knife

Plastic nose with post, 18 (18, 21, 21)mm

Pink acrylic paint

Clear nail polish

Pink felt for tongue and for paw pads on booties and/or handsies

High-temperature (60-watt) hot-glue gun and glue sticks

Round glass bowl vase (page 19)

Pair of solid black eyes, 12mm

Side-cutting needle-nosed pliers

RABBIT HAT

Make a Rolled-Brim Hat (page 28) or Earflap Hat (page 30).

EARS (make 2)

Lay the finished hat flat. With a crochet hook and starting 1 (2, 3, 4) stitch(es) from the center of the top of the hat, pick up 1 stitch. Continuing across the *row*, pick up 3 (3, 4, 4) more stitches, and pick up a 5th (5th, 6th, 6th) stitch on the row *below*. Transfer these stitches to a double-pointed needle. Turn hat over to the back side. With a crochet hook, pick up 4 (4, 5, 5) stitches in the row below the row where you picked up the last stitch on the double-pointed needle. Pick up a 5th (5th, 6th, 6th) stitch 1 row *above*—10 (10, 12, 12) stitches total.

Note: You will be working the ears on two needles, in the round, knitting the back stitches off the crochet hook on the 1st round (see Picking Up Stitches for Ears, page 21).

Round 1: *Ktbl; repeat from * to end of round.

Rounds 2 and 3: Knit.

Round 4: *K2, M1, k3; repeat from * for back needle—12 (12, 14, 14) stitches; 6 (6, 7, 7) stitches on each needle.

Rounds 5 and 6: Knit.

Note: Stuff Ear with polyester fiberfill before continuing to next round.

Round 7: *K3, M1, k3 (3, 4, 4); repeat from * for back needle—14 (14, 16, 16) stitches; 7 (7, 8, 8) stitches on each needle.

Rounds 8 and 9: Knit.

Round 10: *K3 (3, 4, 4), M1, k4; repeat from * for back needle—16 (16, 18, 18) stitches; 8 (8, 9, 9) stitches on each needle.

Rounds 11 and 12: Knit.

Round 13: *K4, M1, k4 (4, 5, 5); repeat from * for back needle—18 (18, 20, 20) stitches; 9 (9, 10, 10) stitches on each needle.

Rounds 14 and 15: Knit.

Round 16: K4 (4, 5, 5), M1, k5; repeat from * for back needle—20 (20, 22, 22) stitches, 10 (10, 11, 11) stitches on each needle.

Rounds 17 and 18: Knit.

Sizes Medium and Large only
Next round: *K5, M1, k6; repeat from * for back needle—24 stitches; 12 stitches on each needle.

All sizes

Next round (decrease round): *K1, k2tog, knit to last 3 stitches on needle, k2tog, k1; repeat from * for back needle—16 (16, 20, 20) stitches; 8 (8, 10, 10) stitches on each needle.

Knit 2 rounds.

Repeat last 3 rounds 2 (2, 3, 3) more times—8 stitches; 4 stitches on each needle.

Next round: K1, k2tog, k1—6 stitches; 3 stitches on each needle.

Cut yarn, and thread through the remaining 6 stitches with blunt-end needle. Weave in end.

CHEEKS

With a double-pointed needle and leaving a 12" (30.5cm) tail for sewing, cast on 21 (21, 27, 27) stitches.

Beginning with a right-side row, work 8 (8, 12, 12) rows in stockinette stitch (knit on RS, purl on WS).

Decrease row (RS): *K1, k2tog; repeat from * to end of row—14 (14, 18, 18) stitches.

Beginning with a wrong-side row, work 3 rows in stockinette stitch.

To bind off, pass all of the stitches over the 1st stitch until 1 stitch remains. Cut yarn, leaving a 6" (15cm) tail for finishing, and thread through the remaining stitch with blunt-end needle.

FINISH CHEEKS

Cut 2 pieces from the 1½ (1½ , 2, 2)" (3.8 [3.8, 5, 5]cm) Styrofoam ball, each ⅛" (3mm) shy of center. Discard the ¼" (6mm) leftover center disk.

Enclose Styrofoam into knit Cheeks, following the directions for Cheeks (page 24).

JAW

Using double-pointed needles, and leaving a 9" (23cm) tail for sewing, knit cast on 12 (12, 18, 18) stitches. Join to work in the round as follows: K3 (3, 4, 4) on 1st needle, k6 (6, 9, 9) stitches on 2nd needle, k3 (3, 5, 5) stitches on 3rd needle.

Using 3rd needle, k3 (3, 4, 4) stitches from 1st needle—6 (6, 9, 9) stitches on each needle.

Knit 2 (2, 4, 4) rounds.

Next round: *K1, k2tog; repeat from * to end of round—8 (8, 12, 12) stitches; 4 (4, 6, 6) on each needle.

Next round: *K2tog; repeat from * to end of round—4 (4, 6, 6) stitches.

Cut yarn and thread through remaining stitches with blunt-end needle. Weave in end.

Follow directions for finishing Jaws (page 24).

FINISH RABBIT HAT

Paint the plastic nose with pink acrylic paint and let dry. Finish with a top coat of clear fingernail polish.

Cut a teardrop shape of pink felt and hot-glue it into the center of the Jaw. Hot-glue the plastic nose in between the Cheeks. Hot-glue the Jaw behind the Cheeks.

Stretch the hat over a glass vase and hot-glue the Cheeks in place. Snip the posts off the eyes and hot-glue in place.

RABBIT BOOTIES (make 2)

Using double-pointed needles, knit cast on 16 (20, 24) stitches.

Join to work in the round as follows: K4 (5, 6) stitches on 1st needle, k8 (10, 12) stitches on 2nd needle, k4 (5, 6) stitches on 3rd needle. Place free needle aside and use 3rd needle to knit 4 (5, 6) stitches from 1st needle—8 (10, 12) stitches on each needle.

Knit 14 (19, 24) rounds.

HEEL FLAP

Note: The heel flap is worked back and forth in rows over the back needle.

Turn work.

Beginning with a wrong-side row, work 7 rows in stockinette stitch (k on RS, p on WS).

Row 8 (RS): Sl 1 knitwise, k3 (5, 7), skp. Turn work.

Row 9 (WS): Sl 1 purlwise, p1 (3, 5), p2tog. Turn work.

Row 10: Sl 1 knitwise, k1 (3, 5), skp. Turn work.

Row 11: Sl 1 purlwise, p1 (3, 5), p2tog. Turn work.

Row 12: Sl 1 knitwise, k1 (3, 5), skp. Turn work—3 (5, 6) stitches.

Row 13: Purl.

Row 14: Knit.

GUSSETS

With back needle, k3 (5, 7) and pick up 5 stitches from the left side of the heel flap (1 stitch in each knot along the top edge).

K8 (10, 12) over the front needle.

With a 3rd needle, pick up 6 stitches along the other side of the heel flap, then k8 (10, 12) from back needle onto this new needle—11 (26, 30) stitches; 8 (10, 12) stitches on the front needle and 14 (16, 18) stitches on the back needle.

Round 1: Knit.

Round 2 (decrease round): Knit across front needle, k1, k2tog, knit to last 3 stitches on back needle, k2tog, k1—2 stitches decreased.

Repeat the last 2 rounds twice more—16 (20, 24) stitches; 8 (10, 12) stitches on each needle.

Knit 4 (11, 19) rounds.

SHAPE FOOT

Sizes Newborn (Small) only
Round 1: *K1, M1, knit to last stitch on needle, M1, k1; repeat from * for back needle—20 (24) stitches; 10 (12) stitches on each needle.

Rounds 2 and 3: Knit.

Size Newborn only
Repeat Rounds 1–3 once more—24 stitches; 12 stitches on each needle.

All sizes
Next round: *K2, ssk, k4, k2tog, k2; repeat from * for back needle—20 stitches; 10 stitches on each needle.

MAKE TOES

Toe 1 (right)
Slip the last 3 stitches on the back needle onto a 3rd needle, then use this 3rd needle to knit the first 3 stitches from the front needle.

Cut yarn, leaving a 36" (91cm) tail, and thread through all 6 stitches with a blunt-end needle. Pull tightly, and thread long tail to bottom of the toe and sew a few stitches across the gap (see Long Ending Tails, page 22). Use tail for remaining toes—14 stitches remain unworked; 7 stitches on each needle.

Toe 2 (left)
K4 on front needle, leaving 3 stitches unworked on front needle.

Use a 3rd needle to k3 remaining stitches on front needle and then k3 from the back needle.

Thread the long tail through all 6 stitches with a blunt-end needle. Pull tightly, and thread tail through to bottom of the toe. Sew a few stitches in the gap as before—8 stitches remain unworked; 4 stitches on each needle.

Toe 3 (middle)

K1 from back needle.

Knit 2 rounds.

Thread the long tail through all 8 stitches with a blunt-end needle. Pull tightly, and thread tail through the toe.

Check between toes to make sure there are no openings left unsewn. Weave in end.

FINISH RABBIT BOOTIES

From pink felt, cut a pair of paw pads (page 154) and hot glue to the bottom of Rabbit Booties.

NEWBORN RABBIT HANDSIES (make 2)

Knit cast on 16 stitches onto double-pointed needles and join in the round as for Rabbit Booties.

Knit 13 rounds.

Shape foot and make toes as for Rabbit Booties.

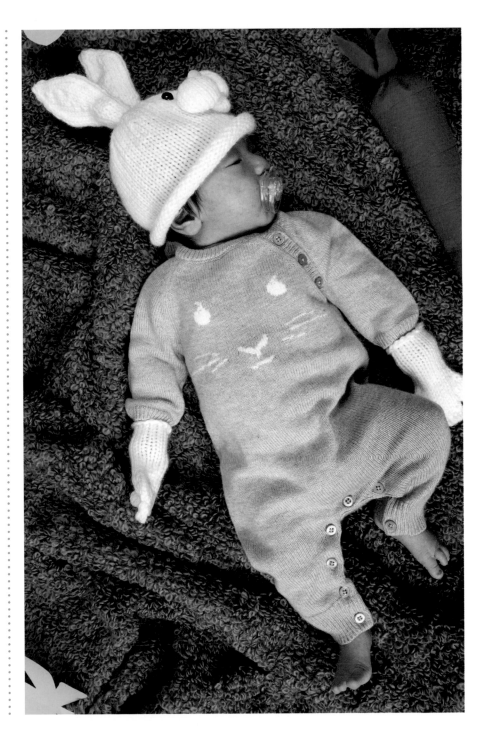

toad

I have made this Gramminal in every shade of green that is available in Vanna's Choice yarns, and I can honestly say that I have never met a green I didn't like. My favorites are Olive and Sweet Pea, but don't let that stop you from trying them all. Sometimes I turn him into a Frog Prince by making him a small, five-point crown based on the Elephant pattern (page 96).

sizes
Newborn (Small, Medium, Large)

finished measurements
13½–16 (15½–18, 17½–20, 19½–22)" (34.5–40.5 [39.5–45.5, 44.5–51, 49.5–56]cm) maximum stretched circumference

gauge
16 stitches and 24 rows = 4" (10cm) in stockinette stitch

materials
For hat: 53 (67, 82, 99) yd (48.5 [61, 75, 90.5]m) / 1 ball Lion Brand Yarn Vanna's Choice, 100% premium acrylic, 3½ oz (100g), 170 yd (156m), in color Olive or Sweet Pea (4)

For hat and booties set: 92, (121, 155, —) yd (84 [110.5, 141.5, —]m) / 1 ball Lion Brand Yarn Vanna's Choice, 100% premium acrylic, 3½ oz (100g), 170 yd (156m), in same color (4)

US size 8 (5mm) 16" (40.5cm) circular needle, or size needed to obtain gauge

Set of 5 US size 8 (5mm) double-pointed needles, or size needed to obtain gauge

Stitch marker

Blunt-end yarn needle

Size F-5 (3.75mm) or G-6 (4mm) crochet hook

Pair of cat eyes, 18mm

Side-cutting needle-nosed pliers

High-temperature (60-watt) hot-glue gun and glue sticks

TOAD STITCH PATTERN
(multiple of 6 stitches)

Rounds 1–3: Knit.

Round 4: *K5, [k1, p1, k1, p1] in the same stitch; repeat from * to end of round.

Round 5: *K5, [sl 3, k1, pass 3 stitches over]; repeat from * to end of round.

Rounds 6–8: Knit.

Round 9: K2, [k1, p1, k1, p1] in the same stitch, *k5, [k1, p1, k1, p1] in the same stitch; repeat from * to last 3 stitches, k3.

Round 10: K2, [sl 3, k1, pass 3 stitches over]; *k5, [sl 3, k1, pass 3 stitches over]; repeat from * to last 3 stitches, k3.

TOAD HAT

Knit cast on 54 (60, 66, 72) stitches.

Knit 1 row.

Place marker and join to work in a round, being careful not to twist the stitches.

Knit 7 rounds.

Work 20 (25, 30, 35) rounds in Toad stitch pattern.

SHAPE CROWN

Note: Switch to double-pointed needles when necessary.

Round 1: *K4, k2tog; repeat from * to end of round—45 (50, 55, 60) stitches.

Rounds 2 and 3: Knit.

Round 4: *K3, k2tog; repeat from * to end of round—36 (40, 44, 48) stitches.

Round 5: K4 (1, 4, 1), [k1, p1, k1, p1] in the same stitch, *k7, [k1, p1, k1, p1] in the same stitch; repeat from * 2 (3, 3, 4) more times, k7 (6, 7, 6).

Round 6: K4 (1, 4, 1), [sl 3, k1, pass 3 stitches over], *k7, [sl 3, k1, pass 3 stitches over]; repeat from * 2 (3, 3, 4) more times, k7 (6, 7, 6).

Round 7: *K2, k2tog; repeat from * to end of round—27 (30, 33, 36) stitches.

Round 8: Knit.

Round 9: K2tog 13 (15, 16, 18) times, k1 (0, 1, 0)—14 (15, 17, 18) stitches.

Round 10: K2tog 7 (7, 8, 9) times, k0 (1, 1, 0)—7 (8, 9, 9) stitches.

Cut yarn, leaving tail for closing. With blunt-end needle, thread tail through remaining stitches. Pull tightly and weave in end.

EYE SOCKET (make 2)

Lay the finished hat flat. With crochet hook and starting at the 3rd (4th, 5th, 6th) stitch from the center of the top of the hat, pick up 7 stitches. Transfer stitches to a double-pointed needle. Turn hat over to the back side. With a crochet hook, pick up 7 stitches directly behind the stitches on the double-pointed needle—14 stitches total.

Note: You will be working the eye socket on 2 needles, in the round, knitting the back stitches off the crochet hook on the 1st round (see Picking Up Stitches for Ears, page 21).

Round 1: *Ktbl; repeat from * to end of round.

Rounds 2–5: Knit.

Round 6: *K2tog; repeat from * to end of round—7 stitches.

Cut yarn, leaving tail for closing. Thread tail through remaining stitches with blunt-end needle. Pull tightly and secure.

FINISH TOAD HAT

Snip the posts off the cat eyes and hot-glue to the center of each Eye Socket.

TOAD BOOTIES (make 2)

Using double-pointed needles, knit cast on 16 (20, 24) stitches.

Join to work in the round as follows: K4 (5, 6) on 1st needle, k8 (10, 12) on

2nd needle, k4 (5, 6) on 3rd needle. Using 3rd needle, k4 (5, 6) from 1st needle—8 (10, 12) stitches on each needle.

Knit 14 (19, 24) rounds.

HEEL FLAP

Note: The heel flap is worked back and forth in rows over the back needle.

Turn work.

Beginning with a wrong-side row, work 7 rows in stockinette stitch (k on RS, p on WS).

Row 8 (RS): Sl 1 knitwise, k3 (5, 7), skp. Turn work.

Row 9 (WS): Sl 1 purlwise, p1 (3, 5), p2tog. Turn work.

Row 10: Sl 1 knitwise, k1 (3, 5), skp. Turn work.

Row 11: Sl 1 purlwise, p1 (3, 5), p2tog. Turn work.

Row 12: Sl 1 knitwise, k1 (3, 5), skp. Turn work—3 (5, 7) stitches.

Row 13: Purl.

Row 14: Knit.

GUSSETS

With back needle, pick up 5 stitches from the left side of the heel flap (1 stitch in each knot along the edge).

K8 (10, 12) over the front needle.

With a 3rd needle, pick up 6 stitches along the other side of the heel flap, then k8 (10, 12) from back needle onto this new needle—22 (26, 30)

stitches; 8 (10, 12) stitches on the front needle and 14 (16, 18) stitches on the back needle.

Round 1: Knit.

Round 2 (decrease round): Knit across front needle; k1, k2tog, knit to last 3 stitches on back needle, k2tog, k1—2 stitches decreased.

Repeat the last 2 rounds twice more—16 (20, 24) stitches; 8 (10, 12) stitches on each needle.

Knit 1 (7, 13) rows.

SHAPE FOOT

Round 1: *K4 (5, 6), M1, k4 (5, 6); repeat from * for back needle—18 (22, 26) stitches; 9 (11, 13) stitches on each needle.

Round 2: *K4 (5, 6), M1, k5 (6, 7); repeat from * for back needle—20 (24, 28) stitches; 10 (12, 14) stitches on each needle.

Round 3: *K5 (6, 7), M1, k5 (6, 7); repeat from * for back needle—22 (26, 30) stitches; 11 (13, 15) stitches on each needle.

Round 4: *K5 (6, 7), M1, k6 (7, 8); repeat from * for back needle—24 (28, 32) stitches; 12 (14, 16) stitches on each needle.

Round 5: *K6 (7, 8), M1, k6 (7, 8); repeat from * for back needle—26 (30, 34) stitches; 13 (15, 17) stitches on each needle.

Round 6: *K6 (7, 8), M1, k7 (8, 9); repeat from * for back needle—28 (32, 36) stitches; 14 (16, 18) stitches on each needle.

Sizes Newborn (Small) only

Round 7: *K7 (8), M1, k7 (8); repeat from * for back needle—30 (34) stitches; 15 (17) stitches on each needle.

Round 8: *K7 (8), M1, k8 (9); repeat from * for back needle—32 (36) stitches; 16 (18) stitches on each needle.

Size Newborn only

Round 9: *K8, M1, k8; repeat from * for back needle—34 stitches; 17 stitches on each needle.

Round 10: *K8, M1, k9; repeat from * for back needle—36 stitches; 18 stitches on each needle.

All sizes

Next round: K2, ssk twice, k3, M1, k3, ssk twice, k2; repeat on back needle—15 stitches on each needle.

FINISH END

Using the 3-needle method (page 150), bind off stitches in the last row in the following pattern, working the stitches on the front and back needles *at the same time*: K2, k2tog, k7, k2tog, k2.

Cut yarn and thread tail through remaining stitch with blunt-end needle. Weave in the end. Use the blunt-end needle to adjust the bound-off stitches at the corners and the center point to accentuate the webbed toes.

NEWBORN TOAD HANDSIES
(make 2)

Knit cast on 16 stitches and join in the round as for Toad Booties.

Knit 10 rounds.

Shape foot and finish end as for Toad Booties.

JUNGLE JUBILEE

monkey

fish

lion

elephant

panda

turtle

monkey

The monkey is very, very special. Though not difficult to make, the construction varies from the other hats with a simple knitted I-cord knotted on top of the crown that looks great on either a Rolled-Brim or Earflap Hat. This Gramminal has a unique oval-shaped face with simple stitched features and matching booties with extra-long toes.

sizes
Newborn (Small, Medium, Large)

finished measurements
13½–16 (15½–18, 17½–20, 19½–22)" (34.5–40.5 [39.5–45.5, 44.5–51, 49.5–56]cm) maximum stretched circumference

gauge
16 stitches and 24 rows = 4" (10cm) in stockinette stitch

materials
For hat: 57 (68, 74, 86) yd (52 [62, 67.5, 78.5]m) / 1 ball Lion Brand Yarn Vanna's Choice, 100% premium acrylic, 3½ oz (100g), 170 yd (156m), in Toffee (A), and 15 (15, 21, 21) yd (14 [14, 19, 19]m) in Honey (B) (4)

For hat and booties set: 95 (123, 156, —) yd (87 [112.5, 142.5, —]m) / 1 ball Lion Brand Yarn Vanna's Choice, 100% premium acrylic, 3½ oz (100g), 170 yd (156m), in Toffee (A), and 15 (15, 21, —) yd (14 [14, 19, —]m) in Honey (B) (4)

US size 8 (5mm) 16" (40.5cm) circular needle, or size needed to obtain gauge

Set of 5 US size 8 (5mm) double-pointed needles, or size needed to obtain gauge

Stitch marker

Blunt-end yarn needle

Size F-5 (3.75mm) or G-6 (4mm) crochet hook

Styrofoam egg, 2⅝ (2⅝, 2⅞, 2⅞)" x 3¹⁄₁₆" (6.5 [6.5, 7.5]cm x 8cm)

Serrated knife

Pair of solid black or animal eyes, 12mm

Side-cutting needle-nosed pliers

High-temperature (60-watt) hot-glue gun and glue sticks

Scrap of black yarn for mouth

Round glass bowl vase (see page 19)

MONKEY HAT

With A, knit a Rolled-Brim Hat (page 28) or Earflap Hat (page 30).

(page 28) or Earflap Hat (page 30).

TOP CURL

With A, a double-pointed needle, and leaving a 6" (15cm) tail for finishing, cast on 3 stitches.

Work these 3 stitches as I-cord (page 150) until it measures approximately 5" (12.5cm) long.

(page 150)

Cut yarn, thread through all 3 stitches with blunt-end needle, and pull tight. Weave in end, leaving tail for finishing.

EARS (make 2)

Lay the finished hat flat. With a crochet hook and starting at the 14th (16th, 18th, 20th) stitch from the center of the top of the hat, pick up 6 stitches along the top edge of the hat. Transfer stitches to a double-pointed needle. Turn hat over to the back side. With a crochet hook, pick up 6 stitches directly behind the stitches on the double-pointed needle—12 stitches total.

Note: You will be working the ears on 2 needles, in the round, knitting the back stitches off the crochet hook on the 1st round (see Picking Up Stitches for Ears, page 21).

(see Picking Up Stitches for Ears, page 21).

Round 1: *Ktbl; repeat from * to end of round.

Round 2: *K1, M1, k4, M1, k1; repeat from * for back needle—16 stitches; 8 stitches on each needle.

Round 3: Knit.

Round 4: *K1, M1, k6, M1, k1; repeat from * for back needle—20 stitches; 10 stitches on each needle.

Round 5: Knit.

Round 6: *K1, k2tog, k4, k2tog, k1; repeat from * for back needle—16 stitches; 8 stitches on each needle.

Round 7: Knit.

Round 8: *K1, k2tog, k2, k2tog, k1; repeat from * for back needle—12 stitches; 6 stitches on each needle.

Round 9: *K1, k2tog twice, k1; repeat from * for back needle—8 stitches; 4 stitches on each needle.

Cut yarn, leaving a tail for finishing, and thread through remaining 8 stitches with blunt-end needle. With the tail, sew a few stitches across the opening so the finished edge is straight. Weave in ends.

EYE SOCKET (make 2)

With B, using double-pointed needles, and leaving a 6" (15cm) tail for finishing, knit cast on 11 (11, 14, 14) stitches.

Knit 1 row.

Beginning with a right-side row, work 4 (4, 6, 6) rows in stockinette stitch (k on RS, p on WS).

To bind off, pass all of the stitches over the 1st stitch until only the 1st stitch remains. Cut yarn, leaving a 6" (15cm) tail, and thread through the remaining stitch, leaving both tails for finishing.

SNOUT

With B, using double-pointed needles, and leaving a 12" (30.5cm) tail for finishing, knit cast on 39 (39, 45, 45) stitches.

Knit 1 row.

Join to work in the round as follows: K9 (9, 10, 10) on 1st needle, k21 (21, 24, 24) on 2nd needle, k9 (9, 11, 11) on 3rd needle. Using 3rd needle, k9 (9, 10, 10) from 1st needle—21 (21, 24, 24) stitches on front needle and 18 (18, 21, 21) stitches on back needle.

Knit 5 (5, 7, 7) rounds.

Next round: *K1, k2tog; repeat from * to end of round—26 (26, 30, 30) stitches; 14 (14, 16, 16) stitches on front needle, 12 (12, 14, 14) stitches on back needle.

Knit 2 rounds.

Next round: *K2tog; repeat from * to end of round—13 (13, 15, 15) stitches; 7 (7, 8, 8) stitches on front needle, 6 (6, 7, 7) stitches on back needle.

Cut yarn and thread through remaining 13 (13, 15, 15) stitches with blunt-end needle. Weave in end, leaving cast-on tail for finishing.

FINISH SNOUT

Cut the Styrofoam egg in half crosswise, and set the round end aside for future projects. Stand the other piece with the pointy side up and cut it in half again, this time through the point. When you lay these two pieces side by side, they create an oval shape.

Enclose Styrofoam into knit Snout, following the directions for Simple Snouts (page 23).

FINISH MONKEY HAT

Sew the Eye Sockets just behind the finished edge of the Snout, shaping them into curves that meet in the middle. Snip posts off the eyes and hot-glue into the Eye Sockets.

Sew the Monkey's mouth and V-shaped nose, following photo, beginning with the stitches between the two pieces of Styrofoam, and ending at the same place (see Stitching a Mouth, page 22).

Stretch the hat over a glass vase and hot-glue the Snout and Eye Sockets in place.

Using the cast-on tail, sew the Top Curl to the center of the top of the hat, and tie into a loose, simple knot.

MONKEY BOOTIES (make 2)

Using double-pointed needles, knit cast on 16 (20, 24) stitches.

Join to work in the round as follows: K4 (5, 6) on 1st needle, k8 (10, 12) on 2nd needle, k4 (5, 6) on 3rd needle. Using 3rd needle, k4 (5, 6) from 1st needle—8 (10, 12) stitches on each needle.

Knit 14 (19, 24) rounds in stockinette stitch.

HEEL FLAP

Note: The heel flap is worked back and forth in rows over the back needle.

Turn work.

Beginning with a wrong-side row, work 7 rows in stockinette stitch (k on RS, p on WS).

Row 8 (RS): Sl 1 knitwise, k3 (5, 7), skp. Turn work.

Row 9 (WS): Sl 1 purlwise, p1 (3, 5), p2tog. Turn work.

Row 10: Sl 1 knitwise, k1 (3, 5), skp. Turn work.

Row 11: Sl 1 purlwise, p1 (3, 5), p2tog. Turn work.

Row 12: Sl 1 knitwise, k1 (3, 5), skp. Turn work—3 (5, 7) stitches.

Row 13: Purl.

Row 14: Knit.

GUSSETS

With back needle, pick up 5 stitches from the left side of the heel flap (1 stitch in each knot along the edge).

K8 (10, 12) over the front needle.

With a 3rd needle, pick up 6 stitches along the other side of the heel flap, then k8 (10, 12) from back needle onto this new needle—22 (26, 30) stitches; 8 (10, 12) stitches on the front needle and 14 (16, 18) stitches on the back needle.

Round 1: Knit.

Round 2: Knit across front needle, k1, k2tog, knit to last 3 stitches on back needle, k2tog, k1—2 stitches decreased.

Repeat the last 2 rounds twice more—16 (20, 24) stitches; 8 (10, 12) stitches on each needle.

Knit 11 (14, 18) rounds.

Size Small only
Next round: *K2, k2tog, k2, ssk, k2; repeat from * for back needle—16 stitches; 8 stitches on each needle.

Size Medium only
Next round: *K1, ssk, k2tog, k2, ssk, k2tog, k1; repeat from * for back needle—16 stitches; 8 stitches on each needle.

MAKE TOES

Note: Outer toes are worked first.

Toe 1 (far right)
Slip the last 2 stitches on the back needle onto a 3rd needle, and use this 3rd needle to knit the first 2 stitches from the front needle.

Work these 4 stitches as I-cord for 5 rounds.

Cut yarn, leaving a 60" (152.5cm) tail, and thread through all 4 stitches with blunt-end needle. Pull tightly and thread long tail through to the bottom of the toe and sew a few stitches across the gap (see Long Ending Tails, page 22). Use tail for remaining toes—12 stitches remain unworked.

Toe 2 (far left)
Knit 4, leaving 2 stitches unworked on front needle.

Use a 3rd needle to knit the last 2 stitches from the front needle and first 2 stitches from the back needle.

Work these 4 stitches as I-cord for 5 rounds.

Thread the long tail through all 4 stitches with blunt-end needle. Pull tightly, and thread tail through the toe and sew a few stitches across the gap as before—8 stitches remain unworked.

Toe 3 (inner right)
K4 on back needle.

Slip the last 2 stitches on the back needle to a 3rd needle, and use this 3rd needle to knit 2 stitches from the front needle.

Work these 4 stitches as I-cord for 5 rounds.

Thread the long tail through all 4 stitches with blunt-end needle. Pull tightly, and thread tail through the toe and sew a few stitches across the gap as before—4 stitches remain unworked.

Toe 4 (inner left)
K2 from front needle, k2 from back needle.

Work these 4 stitches as I-cord for 5 rounds.

Thread the long tail through remaining 4 stitches with blunt-end needle. Weave in end.

Toe-Thumb (work on both booties, opposite sides)
Starting 6 stitches below the base of the outside toe and using a double-pointed needle, pick up 2 stitches. Turn work and pick up 2 corresponding stitches on the back side in the adjacent row.

Work these 4 stitches as I-cord for 5 rounds.

Cut yarn and thread through remaining 4 stitches with blunt-end needle. Weave in end.

NEWBORN MONKEY HANDSIES (make 2)

Knit cast on 16 stitches onto a double-pointed needle and join in the round as for Monkey Booties.

Knit 20 rounds.

Make toes as for Monkey Booties.

fish

This hat came to life simply because Vanna's Choice yarn comes in a color called Goldfish! I highly recommend that this hat be worn sideways so it can be admired fully, even when your child is in a stroller or car seat. And don't be surprised if your little one draws funny comments from complete strangers. As my husband likes to say, "Hey! Who put that fish on your head?"

sizes

Newborn (Small, Medium, Large)

finished measurements

13½–16 (15½–18, 17½–20, 19½–22)" (34.5–40.5 [39.5–45.5, 44.5–51, 49.5–56]cm) maximum stretched circumference

gauge

16 stitches and 24 rows = 4" (10cm) in stockinette stitch

materials

For hat: 71 (85, 102, 119) yd (65 [78, 93.5, 109]m) / 1 ball Lion Brand Yarn Vanna's Choice, 100% premium acrylic, 3½ oz (100g), 170 yd (156m), in Goldfish (4)

For hat and booties set: 115 (145, 181, —) yd (105 [133, 165.5, —]m) / 1, (1, 2, —) ball(s) Lion Brand Yarn Vanna's Choice, 100% premium acrylic, 3½ oz (100g), 170 yd (156m), in Goldfish (4)

US size 8 (5mm) 16" (40.5cm) circular needle, or size needed to obtain gauge

Set of 5 US size 8 (5mm) double-pointed needles, or size needed to obtain gauge

Stitch marker

Blunt-end yarn needle

Stitch holder

Polyester fiberfill

Round glass bowl vase (see page 19)

High-temperature (60-watt) hot-glue gun and glue sticks

Pair of solid black eyes, 12mm

Side-cutting needle-nosed pliers

FISH HAT

Knit a Rolled-Brim Hat (page 28).

TAIL

Using double-pointed needles and leaving an 8" (20.5cm) tail for finishing, knit cast on 8 (8, 10, 10) stitches.

Knit 1 row.

Join to work in the round as follows: K4 (4, 5, 5) stitches on needle 1, k4 (4, 5, 5) stitches on needle 2.

Rounds 1–3: Knit.

Round 4: *K1, M1, k to last stitch on needle, M1, k1; repeat from * for back needle—12 (12, 14, 14) stitches; 6 (6, 7, 7) stitches on each needle.

Round 5: Knit.

Repeat last 2 rounds 3 more times—24 (24, 26, 26) stitches; 12 (12, 13, 13) stitches on each needle.

Sizes Medium and Large only
Next round: *K6, M1, k7; repeat from * for back needle—28 (28) stitches; 14 (14) stitches on each needle.

FIN TIP 1

Round 1: K1, M1, k5 (5, 6, 6), transfer last 6 (6, 7, 7) front needle stitches onto stitch holder, transfer first 6 (6, 7, 7) back needle stitches onto stitch holder, k5 (5, 6, 6), M1, k1—14 (14, 16, 16) stitches; 7 (7, 8, 8) stitches on each needle.

Round 2: K5 (5, 6, 6), ssk, k2tog, k5 (5, 6, 6)—12 (12, 14, 14) stitches; 6 (6, 7, 7) stitches on each needle.

Round 3: K4 (4, 5, 5), ssk, k2tog, k4 (4, 5, 5)—10 (10, 12, 12) stitches; 5 (5, 6, 6) stitches on each needle.

Sizes Medium and Large only
Round 4: K4, ssk, k2tog, k4—10 stitches; 5 stitches on each needle.

All sizes
Next round: *K2tog, k1, ssk; repeat from * for back needle—6 stitches; 3 stitches on each needle.

Next round: K1, ssk, k2tog, k1—4 stitches; 2 stitches on each needle.

Cut yarn, leaving a 48 (48, 60, 60)" (122 [122, 152.5, 152.5]cm) tail and thread through the remaining 4 stitches with blunt-end needle. Pull tightly and thread long tail through to the bottom front stitch of the Fin Tip. Sew a few stitches across the gap (see Long Ending Tails, page 22). Use tail for remaining Fin Tips.

FIN TIP 2

Slip the first 6 (6, 7, 7) stitches from stitch holder onto a double-pointed needle (back), then slip the last 6 (6, 7, 7) stitches from stitch holder onto 2nd double-pointed needle (front).

Round 1: K5 (5, 6, 6), M1, k2, M1, k5 (5, 6, 6)—14 (14, 16, 16) stitches; 7 (7, 8, 8) stitches on each needle.

Round 2: K2tog, k10 (10, 12, 12), ssk—12 (12, 14, 14) stitches; 6 (6, 7, 7) stitches on each needle.

Round 3: K2tog, k8 (8, 10, 10), ssk—10 (10, 12, 12) stitches; 5 (5, 6, 6) stitches on each needle.

Sizes Medium and Large only
Round 4: K2tog, k8, ssk—10 stitches; 5 stitches on each needle.

All sizes
Next round: *K2tog, k1, ssk; repeat from * for back needle—6 stitches; 3 stitches on each needle.

Next round: K2tog, k2, ssk—4 stitches; 2 stitches on each needle.

Cut yarn and thread tail through the remaining 4 stitches with blunt-end needle. Weave in end, leaving cast-on tail for finishing.

TOP FIN

Using double-pointed needles and leaving a 12 (12, 14, 14)" (30.5 [30.5, 35.5, 35.5])cm) tail for finishing, knit cast on 32 (36, 40, 44) stitches.

Knit 1 row.

Join to work in the round as follows: K16 (18, 20, 22) stitches on front needle; k16 (18, 20, 22) stitches on back needle.

Round 1: K1, k2tog, knit to the last stitch on front needle M1, k1; k1, M1, knit to the last 3 stitches on back needle, k2tog, k1.

Round 2: K1, k2tog, knit to last 3 stitches on back needle, k2tog, k1—30 (34, 38, 42) stitches; 15 (17, 19, 21) stitches on each needle.

Round 3: Repeat Round 1.

Round 4: Repeat Round 2—28 (32, 36, 40) stitches; 14 (16, 18, 20) stitches on each needle.

Round 5: K1, k2tog twice, knit to last 3 stitches on front needle, k2tog, k1;

k1, k2tog, knit to last 5 stitches on back needle, k2tog twice, k1—22 (26, 30, 34) stitches; 11 (13, 15, 17) stitches on each needle.

Round 6: K1, k2tog twice, knit to last 5 stitches on back needle, k2tog twice, k1—18 (22, 26, 30) stitches; 9 (11, 13, 15) stitches on each needle.

Round 7: Knit.

Round 8: *K1, k2tog, knit to last 3 stitches on needle, k2tog, k1; repeat from * for back needle—14 (18, 22, 26) stitches; 7 (9, 11, 13) stitches on each needle.

Repeat the last round 1 (2, 3, 4) times—10 stitches; 5 stitches on each needle.

Next round: K1, k2tog, k2 on front needle; k2, k2tog, k1 on back

needle—8 stitches; 4 stitches on each needle.

Last round: K1, k2tog, k1 on front needle; k1, k2tog, k1—6 stitches; 3 stitches on each needle.

Cut yarn and thread through the remaining 6 stitches with a blunt-end needle. Weave in end, leaving cast-on tail for finishing.

FACE

Using double-pointed needles and leaving a 12 (14, 16, 18)" (30.5 [35.5, 40.5, 45.5]cm) tail for finishing, knit cast on 40 (44, 48, 52) stitches.

Knit 1 row.

Join to work in the round as follows: K20 (22, 24, 26) stitches on front

needle, k20 (22, 24, 26) stitches on back needle.

Decrease round: *K1, k2tog, knit to last 3 stitches on needle, k2tog, k1; repeat from * for back needle—36 (40, 44, 48) stitches; 18 (20, 22, 24) stitches on each needle.

Repeat decrease round 7 (8, 9, 10) more times—8 stitches; 4 stitches on each needle.

Next round: K1, k2tog, k2, k2tog, k1—6 stitches; 3 stitches on each needle.

Cut yarn and thread through the remaining 6 stitches with blunt-end needle. Weave in end, leaving tail for finishing.

FINISH TAIL

Stuff the base of the tail with polyester fiberfill, and thread the cast-on tail onto a blunt-end needle. Sew into the bars of the cast-on edge by inserting needle under the first bar from the outside and pulling yarn through. Continue by inserting the needle under the next bar, tightening as you go, until all the cast-on bars have been sewn. Pull to form a nice finished edge on the front and a flat ledge underneath the base that will easily attach to the hat.

FINISH FACE AND TOP FIN

Thread the cast-on tail onto a blunt-end needle and hold the Face or Top Fin with the purl side facing you. Sew into the bars of the cast-on edge by inserting needle under the first bar from the outside and pulling yarn through. Tighten as you sew, just enough to create a nice finished edge on the front of the Face, and a flat ledge underneath that will easily attach to the hat. Weave in end, and stuff lightly with polyester fiberfill.

FINISH FISH HAT

Stretch the hat over a glass vase. Run a bead of hot glue around the flat edges of the Face that will make contact with the hat and hold it in place until it dries. Repeat for the Fin and Tail. Snip the posts on the eyes and glue in place.

Note: If you feel your Face or Top Fin needs a little more stuffing after it has been attached to the hat, add more fiberfill by rolling small pieces into balls and poking them through from the outside with the tip of a double-pointed needle.

FISH BOOTIES (make 2)

Using double-pointed needles, knit cast on 16 (20, 24) stitches.

Join to work in the round as follows: K4 (5, 6) on 1st needle, k8 (10, 12) on 2nd needle, k4 (5, 6) on 3rd needle. Using 3rd needle, k4 (5, 6) from 1st needle—8 (10, 12) stitches on each needle.

Knit 14 (19, 24) rounds.

HEEL FLAP

Note: The heel flap is worked back and forth in rows over the back needle.

Turn work.

Beginning with a wrong-side row, work 7 rows in stockinette stitch (k on RS, p on WS).

Row 8 (RS): Sl 1 knitwise, k3 (5, 7), skp. Turn work.

Row 9 (WS): Sl 1 purlwise, p1 (3, 5), p2tog. Turn work.

Row 10: Sl 1 knitwise, k1 (3, 5), skp. Turn work.

Row 11: Sl 1 purlwise, p1 (3, 5), p2tog. Turn work.

Row 12: Sl 1 knitwise, k1 (3, 5), skp. Turn work—3 (5, 7) stitches.

Row 13: Purl.

Row 14: Knit.

GUSSETS

With back needle, pick up 5 stitches from the left side of the heel flap (1 stitch in each knot along the edge).

K8 (10, 12) stitches over the front needle.

With a 3rd needle, pick up 6 stitches along the other side of the heel flap, then k8 (10, 12) from back needle onto this new needle—22 (26, 30) stitches; 8 (10, 12) stitches on the front needle and 14 (16, 18) stitches on the back needle.

Round 1: Knit.

Round 2: Knit across front needle; k1, k2tog, knit to last 3 stitches on back needle, k2tog, k1—2 stitches decreased.

Repeat last 2 rounds twice more—16 (20, 24) stitches; 8 (10, 12) stitches on each needle.

Knit 8 (10, 12) rounds.

SHAPE TAIL

Round 1: *K1, k2tog, knit to last 3 stitches on needle, k2tog, k1; repeat from * for back needle—12 (16, 20) stitches; 6 (8, 10) stitches on each needle.

Round 2: Knit.

Repeat last 2 rounds 1 (2, 3) more times—8 stitches; 4 stitches on each needle.

Knit 2 rounds.

TAIL FINS

Round 1: *K1, M1, knit to last stitch on needle, M1, k1; repeat from * for back needle—12 stitches; 6 stitches on each needle.

Round 2: Knit.

Repeat last 2 rounds 3 more times—24 stitches; 12 stitches on each needle.

Fin 1

Round 1: K1, M1, k5, transfer last 6 front stitches onto stitch holder, transfer first 6 back stitches onto stitch holder, K5, M1, K1—14 stitches; 7 stitches on each needle.

Round 2: K5, ssk, k2tog, k5—12 stitches; 6 stitches on each needle.

Round 3: K4, ssk, k2tog, k4—10 stitches; 5 stitches on each needle.

Round 4: *K2tog, k1, ssk; repeat from * for back needle—6 stitches; 3 stitches on each needle.

Round 5: K1, ssk, k2tog, k1—4 stitches; 2 stitches on each needle.

Cut yarn, leaving a 48" (122cm) tail and thread through the remaining 4 stitches with blunt-end needle.

Pull tightly and thread long tail through to the front bottom stitch of the Fin Tip. Sew a few stitches across the gap (see Long Ending Tails, page 22). Use tail for Fin 2.

> ›› After designing the Goldfish hat, I couldn't resist adding the tail fin to the end of the booties. When I showed them to my daughter, Jessica, I asked her with some concern, "Have I taken this too far?"
>
> First she laughed out loud, and then, still giggling, she said, "No way, Mom, not for babies that don't even walk yet!"

Fin 2

Slip the first 6 stitches from stitch holder onto a double-pointed needle (back), then slip the last 6 stitches from stitch holder onto 2nd double-pointed needle (front).

Round 1: K5, M1, k2, M1, k5—14 stitches; 7 stitches on each needle.

Round 2: K2tog, k10, ssk—12 stitches; 6 stitches on each needle.

Round 3: K2tog, k8, ssk—10 stitches; 5 stitches on each needle.

Round 4: *K2tog, k1, ssk; repeat from * for back needle—6 stitches; 3 stitches on each needle.

Round 5: K2tog, k2, ssk—4 stitches; 2 stitches on each needle.

Cut yarn and thread tail through the remaining 4 stitches with blunt-end needle. Weave in end.

lion

Inspired by the mascot on the Lion Brand Yarn label, this hat looks incredibly realistic from every angle. He has the most delightful profile and looks great whether he is coming or going—he even looks great worn backward! Each double-loop stitch uses seven times more yarn than a regular knit stitch and requires a multistep process. But—oh!—is it ever worth the time and trouble to learn.

sizes

Newborn (Small, Medium, Large)

finished measurements

13½–16 (15½–18, 17½–20, 19½–22)" (34.5–40.5 [39.5–45.5, 44.5–51, 49.5–56]cm) maximum stretched circumference

gauge

16 stitches and 24 rows = 4" (10cm) in stockinette stitch

materials

For hat: 95 (123, 154, 189) yd (87 [112.5, 141, 173]m) / 1 (1, 1, 2) balls Lion Brand Yarn Vanna's Choice, 100% premium acrylic, 3½ oz (100g), 170 yd (156m), in Mustard (A), and 1½ yd (1.4m) in Lamb (B) **4**

For hat and booties set: 133 (175, 226, —) yd (121.5 [160, 206.5, —]m) / 1 (2, 2, —) balls Lion Brand Yarn Vanna's Choice, 100% premium acrylic, 3½ oz (100g), 170 yd (156m), in Mustard (A), and 1½ yd (1.4m) in Lamb (B) **4**

US size 8 (5mm) 16" (40.5cm) circular needle, or size needed to obtain gauge

Set of 5 US size 8 (5mm) double-pointed needles, or size needed to obtain gauge

Stitch marker

Blunt-end yarn needle

Size F-5 (3.75mm) or G-6 (4mm) crochet hook

Styrofoam ball, 1½" (3.8cm) in diameter

Serrated knife

Scrap of black yarn for mouth

High-temperature (60-watt) hot-glue gun and glue sticks

Black plastic nose with post, 21mm

Round glass bowl vase (see page 19)

Pair of animal eyes, 15mm

Side-cutting needle-nosed pliers

Dark brown felt for paw pads on booties and/or handsies (see Felt Templates, page 154)

SPECIAL STITCHES

Double-Loop Knit

Knit into the next stitch, leaving it on the needle. Bring the yarn forward between the newly created loop on the right needle and the original stitch on the left needle. Place your right thumb on the right needle and wrap the yarn over and around your thumb twice.

With thumb still wrapped, move yarn back between needles and knit into the same stitch as before, this time dropping it off as usual—2 stitches on right needle.

Pass 1st stitch over 2nd stitch, leaving 1 stitch to lock loop in place.

Single-Loop Knit

Work as for Double-Loop Knit, but wrap yarn around thumb only once.

DLk2tog

Knit 2 stitches together while making a double loop.

SLk2tog

Knit 2 stitches together while making a single loop.

LION HAT

Knit cast on 54 (60, 66, 72) stitches.

Row 1: Purl.

Place marker and join to work in the round, being careful not to twist stitches.

Rounds 1 and 3: Knit.

Round 2 and 4: Purl.

Round 5 (decrease round):
*Double-loop knit 7 (8, 9, 10), DLk2tog; repeat from * to end of round—48 (54, 60, 66) stitches.

Round 6: Knit.

Round 7: Double-loop knit to end of round.

Round 8: Knit.

SHAPE FACE OPENING

Round 1: Double-loop knit 5 (7, 9, 11), k12, double-loop knit to end of round.

Round 2 and all even rounds: Knit.

Round 3: Double-loop knit 4 (6, 8, 10), k14, double-loop knit to end of round.

Round 5: Double-loop knit 3 (5, 7, 9), k16, double-loop knit to end of round.

Round 7: Double-loop knit 2 (4, 6, 8), k18, double-loop knit to end of round.

Round 9: Double-loop knit 1 (3, 5, 7), k20, double-loop knit to end of round.

Sizes Small (Medium, Large) only

Round 11: Double-loop knit 2 (4, 6), k22, double-loop knit to end of round.

Round 13: Double-loop knit 1 (3, 5), k24, double-loop knit to end of round.

Sizes Medium (Large) only

Round 15: Double-loop knit 2 (4), k26, double-loop knit to end of round.

Round 17: Double-loop knit 1 (3), k28, double-loop knit to end of round.

Size Large only

Round 19: Double-loop knit 2, k30, double-loop knit to end of round.

Round 21: Double-loop knit 1, k32, double-loop knit to end of round.

SHAPE TOP

Note: Switch to double-pointed needles when necessary.

Round 1: K22 (26, 30, 34), double-loop knit to end of round.

Round 2: *K4, k2tog; repeat from * to end of round—40 (45, 50, 55) stitches.

Round 3: K19 (22, 25, 29), double-loop knit to end of round.

Round 4: *K3, k2tog; repeat from * to end of round—32 (36, 40, 44) stitches.

Round 5: K16 (18, 20, 24), double-loop knit to end of round.

Round 6: *K2, k2tog; repeat from * to end of round—24 (27, 30, 33) stitches.

Round 7: K12 (14, 15, 19), double-loop knit to end of round.

Round 8: SLk2tog to last 0 (1, 0, 1) stitch, single-loop knit 0 (1, 0, 1)—12 (14, 15, 17) stitches.

Round 9: SLk2tog to last 0 (0, 1, 1) stitch, single-loop knit 0 (0, 1, 1)—6 (7, 8, 9) stitches.

Cut yarn, leaving a tail. With a blunt-end needle, thread tail through the remaining 6 (7, 8, 9) stitches. Pull tightly and weave in end.

EARS (make 2)

Lay the finished hat flat. With a crochet hook and working from the center to the side, pick up 8 (8, 10, 10) stitches in the top row of the face opening, where the ear will be. Transfer to a double-pointed needle. Turn hat over to the back side. With a crochet hook, pick up 8 (8, 10, 10) stitches directly behind the stitches on the double-pointed needle—16 (16, 20, 20) stitches total.

Note: You will be working the ears on 2 needles, in the round, knitting the back stitches off the crochet hook on the 1st round (see Picking Up Stitches for Ears, page 21).

Round 1: *Ktbl; repeat from * to end of round.

Round 2: *K1, M1, knit to last stitch on front needle, M1, K1; repeat from * for back needle—20 (20, 24, 24) stitches; 10 (10, 12, 12) stitches on each needle.

Round 3: Knit.

Round 4: *K1, k2tog, k to last 3 stitches on front needle, k2tog, k1; repeat from * for back needle—16 (16, 20, 20) stitches; 8 (8, 10, 10) stitches on each needle.

Round 5: Knit.

Repeat last 2 rounds once (once, twice, twice) more—12 stitches; 6 stitches on each needle.

Next round: *K1, k2tog twice, k1; repeat from * for back needle—8 stitches; 4 stitches on each needle.

Cut yarn, leaving a tail for closing, and thread tail through the remaining 8 stitches with blunt-end needle. Using your ending tail, sew a few stitches across the opening to create a straight finished edge.

CHEEKS

With B, one double-pointed needle, and leaving a 12" (30.5cm) tail for sewing, cast on 21 stitches.

Beginning with a right-side row, work 8 rows in stockinette stitch (knit on RS, purl on WS).

Decrease row (RS): *K1, k2tog; repeat from * to end of round—14 stitches.

Beginning with a wrong-side row, work 3 rows in stockinette stitch.

To bind off, pass all stitches over the 1st until only the 1st stitch remains. Cut yarn, leaving a 6" (15cm) tail for finishing, and thread through the remaining stitch.

FINISH CHEEKS

Cut 2 pieces from the 1½" (3.8cm) Styrofoam ball, each ⅛" (3mm) shy of center. Discard the ¼" (6mm) leftover center disk.

Enclose Styrofoam into knit Cheeks, following the directions for Cheeks (page 24).

NOSE TRIANGLE

With A, double-pointed needles, and leaving a 9" (23cm) tail for finishing, knit cast on 24 stitches. Join to work in the round as follows: K0 on 1st needle, k12 on 2nd needle, k6 on 3rd needle. Using 3rd needle, k6 from 1st needle—12 stitches each needle.

Round 1: Knit.

Round 2: *K1, k2tog, k to last 3 stitches on needle, k2tog, k1; repeat from * for back needle—20 stitches; 10 stitches on each needle.

Round 3: Knit.

Rounds 4–9: Repeat last 2 rounds 3 more times—8 stitches; 4 stitches on each needle.

Round 10: *K1, k2tog, k1; repeat from * to end of round—6 stitches; 3 stitches on each needle.

Cut yarn and thread through the remaining 6 stitches with blunt-end needle. Weave in end.

Follow directions for finishing Nose Triangles (page 24).

FINISH LION HAT

Sew the Lion's mouth on the Cheeks, following the photo, beginning and ending the line of stitches where the plastic nose will be placed (see Stitching a Mouth, page 22).

Hot-glue the black plastic nose above the mouth and the knitted Nose Triangle behind the Cheeks, making sure that the triangle bulges in the center.

Stretch the hat over a glass vase and hot-glue the Nose Triangle and Cheeks into the face opening. Snip the post off the animal eyes and glue in place on either side of the top of the Nose Triangle.

LION BOOTIES (make 2)

Using double-pointed needles, knit cast on 16 (20, 24) stitches.

Join to work in the round as follows: K4 (5, 6) on 1st needle, k8 (10, 12) on 2nd needle, k4 (5, 6) on 3rd needle. Using 3rd needle, k4 (5, 6) from 1st needle—8 (10, 12) stitches on each needle.

Knit 14 (19, 24) rounds.

HEEL FLAP

Note: The heel flap is worked back and forth in rows over the back needle.

Turn work.

Beginning with a wrong-side row, work 7 rows in stockinette stitch (k on RS, p on WS).

Row 8 (RS): Sl 1 knitwise, k3 (5, 7), skp. Turn work.

Row 9 (WS): Sl 1 purlwise, p1 (3, 5), p2tog. Turn work.

Row 10: Sl 1 knitwise, k1 (3, 5), skp. Turn work.

Row 11: Sl 1 purlwise, p1 (3, 5), p2tog. Turn work.

Row 12: Sl 1 knitwise, k1 (3, 5), skp. Turn work—3 (5, 7) stitches.

Row 13: Purl.

Row 14: Knit.

GUSSETS

With back needle, pick up 5 stitches from the left side of the heel flap (1 stitch in each knot along the edge). K8 (10, 12) over the front needle.

With a 3rd needle, pick up 6 stitches along the other side of the heel flap, then k8 (10, 12) from back needle onto this new needle—22 (26, 30) stitches; 8 (10, 12) stitches on the front needle and 14 (16, 18) stitches on the back needle.

Round 1: Knit.

Round 2: Knit across front needle, k1, k2tog, knit to last 3 stitches on back needle, k2tog, k1—2 stitches decreased.

Repeat the last 2 rounds twice more—16 (20, 24) stitches; 8 (10, 12) stitches on each needle.

Knit 1 (7, 15) round(s).

SHAPE FOOT

Round 1: *K1, M1, knit to last stitch on needle, M1, k1; repeat from * for back needle—20 (24, 28) stitches; 10 (12, 14) stitches on each needle.

Rounds 2 and 3: Knit.

Repeat last 3 rounds 2 (1, 0) more time(s)—28 stitches; 14 stitches on each needle.

Next round: *K2, ssk, k6, k2tog, k2; repeat from * for back needle—24 stitches; 12 stitches on each needle.

MAKE TOES

Note: Outer toes are worked first.

Toe 1 (right)

Slip the last 3 stitches on the back needle onto a 3rd needle, then use this 3rd needle to knit the first 3 stitches from the front needle.

Cut yarn, leaving a 42" (106.5cm) tail, and thread through all 6 stitches with blunt-end needle. Pull lightly and thread long tail through to the bottom of the Toe and sew a few stitches across in the gap (see Long Ending Tails, page 22). Use tail for remaining toes—18 stitches remain unworked.

Toe 2 (far left)

On front needle, k6 leaving 3 stitches unworked on front needle.

Use a 3rd needle to knit last 3 stitches from the front needle and k3 stitches from the back needle.

Thread the long tail through all 6 stitches with blunt-end needle. Pull tightly and thread tail through to the bottom of the Toe—12 stitches remain unworked. Sew a few stitches in the gap as before.

Toe 3 (inner right)

K6 on back needle.

Slip the last 3 stitches on the back needle onto a 3rd needle.

Slip the first 3 stitches on front needle onto a 4th needle.

Knit 2 rounds on needles 3 and 4.

Thread the long tail through all 6 stitches with blunt-end needle. Pull tightly and thread tail through to the bottom of the Toe—6 stitches remain unworked. Sew a few stitches in the gap as before.

Toe 4 (inner left)

Knit 2 rounds.

Thread the long tail through all 6 stitches with blunt-end needle. Pull tightly and thread tail through to the bottom of the Toe.

Check between toes to make sure there are no openings left unsewn. Weave in end.

FINISH LION BOOTIES

Cut a pair of paw pads (page 154) from dark brown felt and hot-glue to the bottom of Lion Booties.

NEWBORN LION HANDSIES (make 2)

Knit cast on 16 stitches onto a double-pointed needle and join in the round as for Lion Booties.

Knit 10 rounds.

Round 11: K1, M1, knit to last stitch, M1, k1; repeat on back needle.

Rounds 12 and 13: Knit.

Repeat rounds 11–14 twice more—14 stitches on each needle.

Next round: K2, ssk, k6, k2tog, k2; repeat on back needle—12 stitches on each needle.

Shape foot and make toes as for Lion Booties.

elephant

My nephew Nicholas loved Babar books as a young boy. When he and his wife, Adriane, announced that they were expecting their second child, Elliott, I designed this Gramminal for the newborn. To make sure his big brother felt special, I made him an even better hat, with a double-bend trunk, tusks, and a crown, so he would be the "King of the Elephants." Dad thought they were "the cutest things ever," but Oliver, just turning two, fell madly in love with his, and I saw firsthand for the first time, how truly and dearly a Gramminal can be loved.

sizes
Newborn (Small, Medium, Large)

finished measurements
13½–16 (15½–18, 17½–20, 19½–22)" (34.5–40.5 [39.5–45.5, 44.5–51, 49.5–56]cm) maximum stretched circumference

gauge
16 stitches and 24 rows = 4" (10cm) in stockinette stitch

materials
For hat: 82 (97, 114, 132) yd (75 [88.5, 104, 120.5]m) / 1 ball Lion Brand Yarn Vanna's Choice, 100% premium acrylic, 3½ oz (100g), 170 yd (156m), in Silver Grey (A), 18½ (21, 23½, 26) yd (17 [19, 21.5, 24,]m) in Mustard (B, optional), and 3 (3, 3, 3) yd (3 [3, 3, 3]m) in White (C, optional) (4)

For hat and booties set: 131 (169, 207, —) yd (120 [154.5, 189.5, —]m) / 1 (1, 2, —) balls Lion Brand Yarn Vanna's Choice, 100% premium acrylic, 3½ oz (100g), 170 yd (156m), in Silver Grey (A), 18½ (21, 23½, 26) yd (17 [19, 21.5, 24,]m) in Mustard (B, optional), and 8 (9, 9, —) yd (7.5 [8, 8, —]m) in White (C) (4)

US size 8 (5mm) 16" (40.5cm) circular needle, or size needed to obtain gauge

Set of 5 US size 8 (5mm) double-pointed needles, or size needed to obtain gauge

- Size F-5 (3.75mm) or G-6 (4mm) crochet hook
- Stitch marker
- Blunt-end yarn needle
- Polyester fiberfill
- Round glass bowl vase (see page 19)
- Pair of solid black eyes, 9 (9, 12, 12)mm
- Side-cutting needle-nosed pliers
- High-temperature (60-watt) hot-glue gun and glue sticks
- Styrofoam ball, 2 (2½, 2½, 2½)" (5 [6.5, 6.5]cm) in diameter, for booties
- Serrated knife

ELEPHANT HAT

With A, knit a Rolled-Brim Hat (page 28) or Earflap Hat (page 30).

EARS (make 2)

Lay the finished hat flat. With a crochet hook and starting from the 8th (9th, 10th, 11th) stitch from the center of the top of the hat, pick up 14 (16, 18, 20) stitches along the top edge of the hat. Transfer stitches to a double-pointed needle. Turn hat over to the back side. With a crochet hook, pick up 14 (16, 18, 20) stitches directly behind the stitches on the double-pointed needle—28 (32, 36, 40) stitches total.

Note: You will be working the ears on 2 needles, in the round, knitting the back stitches off the crochet hook on the 1st round (see Picking Up Stitches for Ears, page 21).

Round 1: *Ktbl; repeat from * to end of round.

Round 2: *K1, M1, k to the last stitch on needle, M1, k1; repeat from * for back needle—32 (36, 40, 44) stitches; 16 (18, 20, 22) stitches on each needle.

Round 3: Repeat Round 2—36 (40, 44, 48) stitches; 18 (20, 22, 24) stitches on each needle.

Round 4: Knit.

Round 5: K1, M1, knit to last stitch of back needle, M1, k1—38 (42, 46, 50) stitches; 19 (21, 23, 25) stitches on each needle.

Round 6: Knit to last 2 stitches of front needle, k2tog twice, knit to end of round—36 (40, 44, 48) stitches; 18 (20, 22, 24) stitches on each needle.

Round 7: K1, M1, knit to last 2 stitches of front needle, k2tog; k2tog, knit to last stitch of back needle, M1, k1.

Round 8: Knit to last 2 stitches on front needle, k2tog; k2tog, knit to end of round—34 (38, 42, 46) stitches; 17 (19, 21, 23) stitches on each needle.

Rounds 9 and 10: Work Round 8 twice more—30 (34, 38, 42) stitches; 15 (17, 19, 21) stitches on each needle.

Round 11: *K2tog, knit to last 2 stitches on needle, k2tog; repeat from * for back needle—26 (30, 34, 38) stitches; 13 (15, 17, 19) stitches on each needle.

Round 12: Knit to last 4 stitches on front needle, k2tog twice; k2tog twice, knit to end of round—22 (26, 30, 34) stitches; 11 (13, 15, 17) stitches on each needle.

Round 13: Repeat Round 12—18 (22, 26, 30) stitches; 9 (11, 13, 15) stitches on each needle.

>> The Elephant is very near and dear to my heart—not only because he was the Grand Prize Winner of the 2012 Vanna's Choice Contest but also because the elephant is the official mascot of the USS *Alabama*. Roll Tide!

Round 14: K2tog, knit to last 2 stitches, k2tog—16 (20, 24, 28) stitches; 8 (10, 12, 14) stitches on each needle.

Round 15: Knit.

Round 16 (decrease round): *K2tog, knit to the last 2 stitches on needle, k2tog; repeat from * for back needle—12 (18, 20, 24) stitches, 8 (8, 10, 12) stitches on each needle.

Round 17: K2tog, knit to last 2 stitches, k2tog—10 (14, 18, 22) stitches; 5 (7, 9, 11) stitches on each needle.

Repeat Round 16 (decrease round) 0 (1, 2, 3) time(s) more—10 stitches; 5 stitches on each needle. Cut yarn and thread through the remaining 10 stitches with blunt-end needle. With tail, sew a few stitches across the opening, creating a straight finished edge.

TRUNK

Using double-pointed needles and leaving a 9" (23cm) tail for finishing, knit cast on 21 stitches.

Knit 1 row.

Join to work in the round as follows: K4 on 1st needle, k12 on 2nd needle, k5 on 3rd needle. Using 3rd needle, k4 from 1st needle—12 stitches on front needle, 9 stitches on back needle.

Round 1: Knit.

Round 2: *K1, k2tog; repeat from * to end of round—14 stitches; 8 stitches on front needle, 6 stitches on back needle.

Round 3: K7, wrap and turn (see page 153), p6, wrap and turn, k6, knit wrap together with the next stitch, k6.

Round 4: Knit wrap together with the 1st stitch, k5, wrap and turn, p4, wrap and turn, k4, knit wrap together with the next stitch, k7.

Round 5: K1, knit wrap together with the next stitch, k12.

Rounds 6–8: Repeat Rounds 3–5.

Round 9: K2, k2tog twice, k3, k2tog twice, k1—10 stitches; 6 stitches on front needle, 4 stitches on back needle.

Round 10: K5, wrap and turn, p4, wrap and turn, k4, knit wrap together with the next stitch, k4.

Round 11: Knit wrap together with the 1st stitch, k3, wrap and turn, p2, wrap and turn, k2, knit wrap together with the next stitch, k5.

Round 12: K1, knit wrap together with the next stitch, k8.

Rounds 13–15: Repeat Rounds 10–12.

Note: If you are making a Single-Bend Trunk, skip to Round 19.

Double-Bend Trunk only (as seen on Elephant Hat with Crown)

Round 16: K1 and slip that stitch onto the back needle. With a 3rd needle, k4—1 stitch remaining on front needle. With a 4th needle, knit 1 remaining stitch, k4, wrap and turn, p4, wrap and turn, k4, knit wrap together with the next stitch.

Round 17: K4, knit wrap together with the next stitch, k3, wrap and turn, p2, wrap and turn, k2, knit wrap together with the next stitch, k1.

Round 18: K5, knit wrap together with the next stitch, k4.

Both Trunk Styles

Rounds 19 and 20: Knit.

Round 21: Bind off 9 stitches—1 stitch remains.

Cut yarn, leaving 8" (20.5cm) tail for sewing, pull thread through the remaining stitch with a blunt-end needle.

FINISH TRUNK

Stuff Trunk lightly with polyester fiberfill. Thread the cast-on tail onto a blunt-end needle and hold the Trunk with the base facing you. Sew into the bars of the cast-on edge by inserting needle under the 1st bar from the outside and pulling yarn through. Continue by inserting the needle under the next bar tightening as you go, until all of the cast-on bars have been sewn. Pull to form a nice finished edge on the outside of the Trunk and a flat ledge underneath the base of the Trunk that will easily attach to the hat. Weave in end.

Using the ending tail, sew through the inside loops of the bind-off edge to finish the top of the Trunk.

TUSKS (make 2)

With B, using double-pointed needles, and leaving a 6" (15cm) tail for sewing, knit cast on 6 (8, 8, 8) stitches.

Beginning with a right-side row, work 2 rows in stockinette stitch (knit on RS, purl on WS).

Next row (RS): K2tog 3 (3, 4, 4) times—3 (3, 4, 4) stitches.

Work these 3 (3, 4, 4) stitches as I-cord (page 150) for 4 rounds.

Sizes Small, Medium, and Large only

Next round: K2tog twice in I-cord—2 stitches.

All sizes

Cut yarn, thread tail through remaining stitches with blunt-end needle, pull tightly, and weave in end.

With cast-on tail, create a finished edge by sewing into the bars of the cast-on edge by inserting needle under the 1st bar from the outside and pulling through. Sew the first 3 rows closed at the base of the trunk. Weave in end.

CROWN

Notes: Crown is worked back and forth in rows. The finished Crown has 7 (8, 9, 10) points.

With B, knit cast on 3 stitches.

Row 1: Knit.

Row 2: K2, kfb—4 stitches.

Row 3: Kfb, k3—5 stitches.

Row 4: K4, kfb—6 stitches.

Row 5: Kfb, k5—7 stitches.

Row 6: K6, kfb—8 stitches

Row 7: Bind off 5 stitches, 1 stitch remains on the needle, k2—3 stitches.

Row 8: Knit.

Repeat Rows 1–8 above 12 (14, 16, 18) more times, until you have made 13 (15, 17, 19) points.

Repeat Rows 1–6.

Bind off all stitches. Cut yarn, leaving a tail for sewing, and pull through the remaining stitch.

Fold Crown in half and sew up and down the points at the top, making a double-thick Crown. Lightly stuff each point with fiberfill.

Note: If you elect to sew the Crown to the top of the hat, sew around the inside edge first, then the outside edge ½" (13mm) farther out.

FINISH ELEPHANT HAT

Trim the post from the back of the eyes. Stretch the hat on round glass vase and hot-glue the Elephant's Trunk, then glue on the eyes above the Trunk, and glue the Tusks on either side of the base of the Trunk.

ELEPHANT BOOTIES (make 2)

With A and using double-pointed needles, knit cast on 16 (20, 24) stitches.

Join to work in the round as follows: K4 (5, 6) on 1st needle, k8 (10, 12) on 2nd needle, k4 (5, 6) on 3rd needle. Using 3rd needle, k4 (5, 6) stitches from 1st needle—8 (10, 12) stitches on each needle.

Knit 14 (19, 24) rounds.

HEEL FLAP

Note: The heel flap is worked back and forth in rows over the back needle.

Turn work.

Beginning with a wrong-side row, work 7 rows in stockinette stitch (k on RS, p on WS).

Row 8 (RS): Sl 1 knitwise, k3 (5, 7), skp. Turn work.

Row 9 (WS): Sl 1 purlwise, p1 (3, 5), p2tog. Turn work.

Row 10: Sl 1 knitwise, k1 (3, 5), skp. Turn work.

Row 11: Sl 1 purlwise, p1 (3, 5), p2tog. Turn work.

Row 12: Sl 1 knitwise, k1 (3, 5), skp. Turn work—3 (5, 7) stitches.

Row 13: Purl.

Row 14: Knit.

GUSSETS

With back needle, pick up 5 stitches from the left side of the heel flap

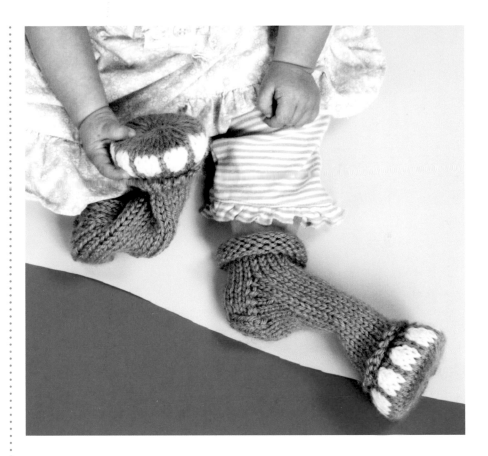

(1 stitch in each knot along the top edge).

K8 (10, 12) stitches over the front needle.

With a 3rd needle, pick up 6 stitches along the other side of the heel flap, then k8 (10, 12) from back needle onto this new needle—22 (26, 30) stitches; 8 (10, 12) stitches on the front needle and 14 (16, 18) stitches on the back needle.

Round 1: Knit.

Round 2: Knit across front needle; k1, k2tog, knit to last 3 stitches on

back needle, k2tog, k1—2 stitches decreased.

Repeat the last 2 rounds twice more—16 (20, 24) stitches; 8 (10, 12) stitches on each needle.

Knit 11 (15, 19) rounds.

Purl 1 round.

Knit 2 (1, 1, 1) rounds.

Size Small only

Next round: *K2, k2tog, k2, ssk, k2; repeat from * for back needle—16 stitches; 8 stitches on each needle.

around the nonworking yarn to secure. After working Round 1, it is helpful to cut B, leaving a 60" (75", 75") (155.5 [190.5, 190.5]cm) tail to continue knitting.

Rounds 1–3: * K1 with A, k3 with B; repeat from * to end of round.

Cut B and knot cast-on and ending tails together.

Round 4: With A, *k1, k3tog; repeat from * to end of round—16 (20, 20) stitches.

Knit 2 (4, 4) rounds.

Final round: K2tog to end—8 (10, 10) stitches.

Cut yarn and thread through the remaining 8 (10, 10) stitches with blunt-end needle. Weave in end.

FINISH ELEPHANT BOOTIES

Cut the Styrofoam ball in half. Thread cast-on tail onto a blunt-end needle and hold Foot with the purl side facing you. Place one half of the Styrofoam ball into the purl side, centering the flat side of the Styrofoam against the knit base. Close the opening by sewing into the cast-on bar by inserting blunt-end needle under the 1st bar from the outside and pulling through tightly. Continue sewing the cast-on bars until ball has been closed in as tightly as possible. Weave in end. (See Snouts, page 23.) Run a bead of hot glue around the inside of the flat edge of the bootie and attach to the Foot.

Size Medium only

Next round: *K1, ssk, k2tog, k2, ssk, k2tog, k1; repeat from * for back needle—16 stitches; 8 stitches on each needle.

All sizes

Next round: *K2, k2tog; repeat from * to end of round—12 stitches; 6 stitches on each needle.

Last round: *K2tog; repeat from * to end of round—6 stitches; 3 stitches on each needle.

Cut yarn and thread through the remaining 6 stitches with blunt-end needle. Weave in end.

FOOT (make 2)

With A, using double-pointed needles, and leaving a 10" (25.5cm) tail for sewing, knit cast on 16 (20, 20) stitches.

Row 1 (RS): *Kfb; repeat from * to end of row—32 (40, 40) stitches.

Row 2 (WS): Purl.

Join to work in the round as follows: K8 (12, 12) on 1st needle, k16 (20, 20) on 2nd needle, k8 onto 3rd needle. Using 3rd needle, k8 (12, 12) from 1st needle—16 (20, 20) stitches on the front needle and 16 (20, 20) stitches on the back needle.

Note: When changing colors in first 3 rounds, twist the working yarn

panda

I have lost track of how many times people have asked me to knit this design. Pandas are universally beloved, and you will definitely get a few requests of your own! Unlike the Bear (page 38), the Panda's ears have a straight edge, created by a special bind-off technique. To make sure that both ears finish the same, you will pick up each ear starting on the same side of the hat.

sizes
Newborn (Small, Medium, Large)

finished measurements
13½–16 (15½–18, 17½–20, 19½–22)" (34.5–40.5 [39.5–45.5, 44.5–51, 49.5–56]cm) maximum stretched circumference

gauge
16 stitches and 24 rows = 4" (10cm) in stockinette stitch

materials
For hat: 56 (68, 84, 100) yd (51 [62, 77, 91.5]m) / 1 ball Lion Brand Yarn Vanna's Choice, 100% premium acrylic, 3½ oz (100g), 170 yd (156m), in White (A), and 14 yd (12.8m) in Black (B) (4)

For hat and booties set: 59 (71, 87, —) yd (54 [65, 80, —]m) / 1 ball Lion Brand Yarn Vanna's Choice, 100% premium acrylic, 3½ oz (100g), 170 yd (156m), in White (A), and 47 (63, 83, —) yd (43 [57.5, 76, —]m) in Black (B) (4)

US size 8 (5mm) 16" (40.5cm) circular needle, or size needed to obtain gauge

Set of 5 US size 8 (5mm) double-pointed needles, or size needed to obtain gauge

Stitch marker

Blunt-end yarn needle

Size F-5 (3.75mm) or G-6 (4mm) crochet hook

Styrofoam ball, 2 (2, 2½, 2½)" (5, [5, 6.5, 6.5]cm) in diameter

Serrated knife

Scrap of black yarn for mouth

Pair of animal eyes, 12mm

Side-cutting needle-nosed pliers

High-temperature (60-watt) hot-glue gun and glue sticks

Black plastic nose with post, 21mm

Round glass bowl vase (see page 19)

PANDA HAT

With A, knit a Rolled-Brim Hat (page 28) or Earflap Hat (page 30).

EARS (make 2)

Lay the finished hat flat. With a crochet hook and B, start at the 4th stitch from the center of the top of the hat and pick up 4 stitches. Transfer to a double-pointed needle. Turn hat over to the back side. With a crochet hook, pick up 4 stitches directly behind the stitches on the double-pointed needle—8 stitches total.

Note: You will be working the ears on 2 needles, in the round, knitting the back stitches off the crochet hook on the 1st round (see Picking Up Stitches for Ears, page 21).

Note: When picking up for the 2nd ear, pick up 4 stitches, starting 8 stitches from the center and ending 4 stitches from the center.

Round 1: *Ktbl; repeat from * to end of round.

Round 2: Knit.

Round 3: *K2, M1, k2; repeat from * for back needle—10 stitches; 5 stitches on each needle.

Round 4: *K1, M1, k3, M1, k1; repeat from * for back needle—14 stitches; 7 stitches on each needle.

Round 5: *K3, M1, k4; repeat from * for back needle—16 stitches; 8 stitches on each needle.

Round 6: *K1, M1, k6, M1, k1; repeat from * for back needle—20 stitches; 10 stitches on each needle.

Round 7: *K5, M1, k5; repeat from * for back needle—22 stitches; 11 stitches on each needle.

Round 8: *K5, M1, k6; repeat from * for back needle—24 stitches; 12 stitches on each needle.

Round 9: Knit.

Round 10: *K1, k2tog, k6, k2tog, k1; repeat from * for back needle—20 stitches; 10 stitches on each needle.

Round 11: *K1, k2tog, k4, k2tog, k1; repeat from * for back needle—16 stitches; 8 stitches on each needle.

Round 12: *K1, k2tog, k2, k2tog, k1; repeat from * for back needle—12 stitches; 6 stitches on each needle.

Bind off by knitting into both stitches on the front and back needle at the same time like for a 3-needle bind-off (page 150), passing the 1st knitted stitch on the right needle over the 2nd knitted stitch on the right needle.

Weave in end.

SNOUT

With A, using double-pointed needles, and leaving a 12" (30.5cm) tail for finishing, knit cast on 30 (30, 33, 33) stitches.

Knit 1 row.

Join to work in the round as follows: K6 (6, 7, 7) on 1st needle, k18 on 2nd needle, k6 (6, 8, 8) on 3rd needle. Using 3rd needle, k6 (6, 7, 7) from 1st needle—18 stitches on front needle; 12 (12, 15, 15) stitches on back needle.

Knit 3 (3, 5, 5) rounds.

Round 1: *K1, k2tog; repeat from * to end of round—20 (20, 22, 22) stitches; 12 stitches on front needle, 8 (8, 10, 10) stitches on back needle.

Round 2: Knit.

Round 3: *K2tog; repeat from * to end of round—10 (10, 11, 11) stitches; 6 stitches on front needle, 4 (4, 5, 5) stitches on back needle.

Cut yarn and thread through remaining 10 (10, 11, 11) stitches with blunt-end needle. Weave in end.

FINISH SNOUT

Cut the Styrofoam ball in half.

Enclose a Styrofoam half into knit Snout, following the directions for Simple Snouts (page 23).

EYE PATCH (make 2)

With B, one double-pointed needle, and leaving a 12" (30.5cm) tail, knit cast on 10 stitches.

Row 1: Knit.

Rows 2–5: Beginning with a right-side row, work 4 rows in stockinette stitch (knit on RS, purl on WS).

To bind off, pass all of the stitches over the 1st stitch until only the 1st stitch remains. Cut yarn, and thread through the remaining stitch.

Thread the cast-on tail onto a blunt-end needle and hold the Eye Patch purl side up. Sew into the bars of the cast-on edge by inserting needle under the bar from the outside and pulling through. Pull tight to create a finished edge on the knit side.

FINISH PANDA HAT

Sew the Panda's mouth, following photo, beginning and ending the line of stitches where the nose will be placed (see Stitching a Mouth, page 22).

Snip the posts off the eyes and hot-glue them high up on the Eye Patches.

With a double-pointed needle, make a hole in the center of the Snout to fit the post on the back of the plastic nose. Hot-glue the nose into and around the hole, making sure that the hot glue bonds the yarn to the back of the nose (see Plastic Animal Noses, page 18).

Stretch the hat over a glass vase. Attach the Snout with hot glue. Hot-glue the Eye Patches on either side of the Snout.

PANDA BOOTIES (make 2)

With B and using double-pointed needles, knit cast on 16 (20, 24) stitches.

Join to work in the round as follows: K4 (5, 6) on 1st needle, k8 (10, 12) on 2nd needle, k4 (5, 6) on 3rd needle. Using 3rd needle, k4 (5, 6) from 1st needle—8 (10, 12) stitches on each needle.

Knit 14 (19, 24) rounds.

HEEL FLAP

Note: The heel flap is worked back and forth in rows over the back needle.

Turn work.

Beginning with a wrong-side row, work 7 rows in stockinette stitch (k on RS, p on WS).

Row 8 (RS): Sl 1 knitwise, k3 (5, 7), skp. Turn work.

Row 9 (WS): Sl 1 purlwise, p1 (3, 5), p2tog. Turn work.

Row 10: Sl 1 knitwise, k1 (3, 5), skp. Turn work.

Row 11: Sl 1 purlwise, p1 (3, 5), p2tog. Turn work.

Row 12: Sl 1 knitwise, k1 (3, 5), skp. Turn work—3 (5, 7) stitches.

Row 13: Purl.

Row 14: Knit.

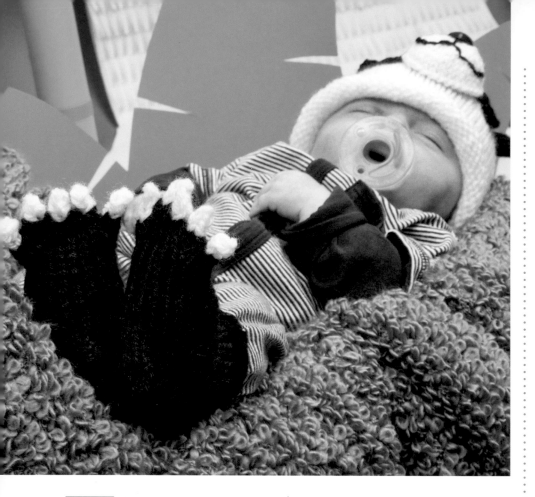

Size Medium only

Next round: *K2, k2tog, k2, ssk, k2; repeat from * for back needle—20 stitches; 10 stitches each needle.

All sizes

Next round: K18, leaving 2 stitches remaining unworked on back needle. *Do not cut B.*

MAKE CLAWS

Note: Outer claws are worked first.

Claw 1 (far right)

With A and a 3rd needle, k2tog on back needle (the remaining 2 unworked stitches), then k2tog from front needle.

Work these 2 stitches as I-cord (page 150) for 2 rounds.

Cut A, leaving 4" (10cm) tail, and thread through 2 stitches with blunt-end needle.

Claw 2 (far left)

With B, k6 on front needle, leaving 2 stitches remaining unworked.

With A and 3rd needle, k2tog on front needle (the remaining 2 unworked stitches), then k2tog on back needle.

Work these 2 stitches as I-cord for 2 rounds.

Cut A, leaving 4" (10cm) tail, and thread through 2 stitches with blunt-end needle.

GUSSETS

With back needle, pick up 5 stitches from the left side of the heel flap (1 stitch in each knot along the edge).

K8 (10, 12) stitches over the front needle.

With a 3rd needle, pick up 6 stitches along the other side of the heel flap, then k8 (10, 12) from back needle onto this new needle—22 (26, 30) stitches; 8 (10, 12) stitches on front needle and 14 (16, 18) stitches on back needle.

Round 1: Knit.

Round 2: Knit across front needle, k1, k2tog, knit to last 3 stitches on back needle, k2tog, k1—2 stitches decreased.

Repeat the last 2 rounds twice more—16 (20, 24) stitches; 8 (10, 12) stitches on each needle.

Knit 9 (14, 17) rounds.

Size Newborn only

Next round: *K2, M1, k4, M1, k2; repeat from * for back needle—20 stitches; 10 stitches each needle.

Claw 3 (inner right)

With B, k4 on back needle, leaving 2 stitches remaining unworked.

With A and 3rd needle, k2tog on back needle (the remaining 2 unworked stitches), then k2tog on front needle.

Work these 2 stitches as I-cord for 2 rounds.

Cut A, leaving 4" (10cm) tail, and thread through 2 stitches with blunt-end needle.

Claw 4 (inner left)

With B, k2 on front needle, leaving 2 stitches remaining unworked.

With A and 3rd needle, k2tog on front needle (the remaining 2 stitches), then k2tog on back needle.

Work these 2 stitches as I-cord for 2 rounds.

Cut A, leaving 4" (10cm) tail, and thread through 2 stitches with blunt-end needle.

Claw 5 (middle)

With B, k2 on back needle. Cut B, leaving 12" (30.5cm) tail for sewing.

With A, and a 3rd needle, k2tog twice.

Work these 2 stitches as I-cord for 2 rounds.

Cut A, leaving 4" (10cm) tail, and thread through 2 stitches with blunt-end needle.

FINISH PANDA BOOTIES

With 12" (30.5cm) tail of B, close any openings between claws.

Turn bootie inside out and tie all the loose ends of A together with double or triple knots.

Trim ends to ¼" (6mm).

NEWBORN PANDA HANDSIES (make 2)

With A, knit cast on 16 stitches onto a double-pointed needle and join in the round as for Panda Booties.

Knit 18 rounds.

Next round: K2, M1, k4, M1, k2—10 stitches each needle.

Next round: K18, leaving 2 stitches unworked on back needle.

Make claws as for Panda Booties.

turtle

This hat is a showstopper, featuring a fun-to-knit stitch pattern on its shell and a little bit of easy color work. It's the cutest introduction to stranded color knitting ever (page 153). Don't be surprised to see your child dragging the Turtle around the house by its flipper and playing with the hat as though it were a stuffed animal. With extra-special details (including a tail), it's practically a toy!

sizes
Newborn (Small, Medium, Large)

finished measurements
13½–16 (15½–18, 17½–20, 19½–22)" (34.5–40.5 [39.5–45.5, 44.5–51, 49.5–56]cm) maximum stretched circumference

gauge
16 stitches and 24 rows = 4" (10cm) in stockinette stitch

materials
For hat: 15 (23, 32, 42) yd (14 [21, 29.5, 38.5]m) / 1 ball Lion Brand Yarn Vanna's Choice, 100% premium acrylic, 3½ oz (100g), 170 yd (156m), in Aqua (A), 38 (38, 41, 41) yd (34.5 [34.5, 37.5, 37.5]m) / 1 ball in Sweet Pea (B), and 29 (32, 36, 39) yd (26.5 [29.5, 33, 35.5]m) / 1 ball in Kelly Green (C) (4)

For hat and booties set: 15 (23, 32, —) yd (14 [21, 29.5, —]m) / 1 ball Lion Brand Yarn Vanna's Choice, 100% premium acrylic, 3½ oz (100g), 170 yd (156m), in Aqua (A), 72 (89, 108, —) yd (66 [81.5, 99, —]m) / 1 ball in Sweet Pea (B), and 29 (32, 36, —) yd (26.5 [29.5, 33, —]m) / 1 ball in Kelly Green (C) (4)

US size 8 (5mm) 16" (40.5cm) circular needle, or size needed to obtain gauge

Set of 5 US size 8 (5mm) double-pointed needles, or size needed to obtain gauge

Stitch marker

Blunt-end yarn needle

Polyester fiberfill

Round glass bowl vase (see page 19)

High-temperature (60-watt) hot-glue gun and glue sticks

Pair of solid black eyes, 6 (6, 9, 9)mm

Side-cutting needle-nosed pliers

TURTLE HAT

With A, knit cast on 54 (60, 66, 72) stitches.

Knit 1 row.

Place marker and join to work in the round, being careful not to twist stitches.

Knit 9 (13, 17, 21) rounds.

Cut A and join B.

With B, knit 2 rounds.

Note: The next 3 rounds are worked in stranded color knitting (page 153) with B and C. The M1Ps are made on strands of yarn that match the color of the working yarn. In order to make the first M1P possible on

round 2, you will need to tie your beginning tail to the last same-color stitch from round 1.

Round 1: *K1 in C, k5 in B; repeat from * to end of round.

Round 2: *With C, M1P, p1, M1P, with B, k2tog, k1, k2tog; repeat from * to end of round.

Round 3: *With C, M1P, k3, M1P, with B, k3tog; repeat from * to end of round.

Cut B, and continue with C.

TURTLE SHELL

Round 4: Knit.

Rounds 5–7: *K5, p1; repeat from * to end of round.

Round 8: *K2tog, k1, k2tog, M1P, p1, M1P; repeat from * to end of round.

Round 9: *K3tog, M1P, k3, M1P; repeat from * to end of round.

Rounds 10–13: *P1, k5; repeat from * to end of round.

Round 14: *M1P, p1, M1P, k2tog, k1, k2tog; repeat from * to end of round.

Round 15: *M1P, k3, M1P, k3tog; repeat from * to end of round.

Rounds 16–19: *K5, p1; repeat from * to end of round.

SHAPE CROWN

Note: Switch to double-pointed needles when necessary.

Round 1: *K2tog, k1, k2tog, p1; repeat from * to end of round—36

(40, 44, 48) stitches.

Round 2: *P3tog, M1P, p1; repeat from * to end of round—27 (30, 33, 36) stitches.

Knit 1 (1, 2, 2) rounds.

Next round: *K1, k2tog; repeat from * to end of round—18 (20, 22, 24) stitches.

Next round: *K2tog; repeat from * to end of round—9 (10, 11, 12) stitches.

Cut yarn, leaving tail for closing. With blunt-end needle, thread tail through remaining stitches. Pull tightly and weave in end.

HEAD

With B, using double-pointed needles, and leaving a 9" (23cm) tail for sewing, knit cast on 12 stitches.

Knit 1 row.

Join to work in the round as follows: K3 on 1st needle, k6 on 2nd needle, k3 on 3rd needle. Using 3rd needle, k3 from 1st needle—6 stitches on each needle.

Round 1: Knit.

Round 2: K1, M1, knit to last stitch on needle, M1, k1; repeat from * for back needle—16 stitches; 8 stitches on each needle.

Repeat last round 2 (2, 3, 3) times—24 (24, 28, 28) stitches; 12 (12, 14, 14) stitches on each needle.

Knit 2 rounds.

Next round: *K1, k2tog, knit to the

last 3 stitches on needle, k2tog, k1; repeat from * for back needle—4 stitches decreased.

Repeat last round 3 (3, 4, 4) times—8 stitches; 4 stitches on each needle.

Next round: *K1, k2tog, k1; repeat from * for back needle—6 stitches; 3 stitches on each needle.

Cut yarn and thread tail through remaining 6 stitches with blunt-end needle. Pull tightly and weave in end, leaving cast-on tail for finishing.

TAIL

With B, using double-pointed needle, and leaving a 9" (23cm) tail for sewing, knit cast on 8 stitches.

Knit 1 row.

Join to work in the round as follows: K2 on 1st needle, k4 on 2nd needle, k2 on 3rd needle. Using 3rd needle, k2 from 1st needle—4 stitches on front needle and 4 stitches on back needle.

Rounds 1 and 2: Knit.

Round 3: *K1, k2tog, k1; repeat from * for back needle—6 stitches; 3 stitches on each needle.

Rounds 4 and 5: Knit.

Round 6: *K1, k2tog; repeat from * for back needle—4 stitches; 2 stitches on each needle.

Round 7: K2tog twice—2 stitches; 1 stitch on each needle.

Cut yarn and thread through remaining 2 stitches with blunt-end needle. Weave in end, leaving cast-on tail for finishing.

BACK LEGS (make 2)

With B, using double-pointed needles, and leaving a 9" (23cm) tail for sewing, knit cast on 14 stitches.

Knit 1 row.

Join to work in the round as follows: K3 on 1st needle, k8 on 2nd needle, k3 on 3rd needle. Using 3rd needle, k3 stitches from 1st needle—8 stitches on front needle and 6 stitches on back needle.

Round 1: Knit.

Round 2: K2, k2tog twice, k2 on front needle, k1, k2tog twice, k1 on back needle—10 stitches; 6 stitches on front needle, 4 stitches on back needle.

Rounds 3 and 4: Knit.

Round 5: K5, wrap and turn (see page 153), p4, wrap and turn, k4, knit wrap together with next stitch, k4.

Round 6: Knit wrap together with 1st stitch, k9.

Round 7: K4, wrap and turn, p2, wrap and turn, k2, knit wrap together with next stitch, k5.

Round 8: K1, knit wrap together with next stitch, k8.

Rounds 9–11: Knit.

Cut yarn and thread through the remaining 10 stitches with blunt-end needle. Weave in end, leaving cast-on tail for finishing.

FRONT FLIPPER (make 2)

Follow instructions for Back Legs through round 4.

Round 5: K5, wrap and turn, p4, wrap and turn, k4, knit wrap together with the stitch, k4.

Round 6: Knit wrap together with 1st stitch, k3, wrap and turn, p2, wrap and turn, k2, knit wrap together with next stitch, k5.

Round 7: K1, knit wrap together with next stitch, k3, wrap and turn, p4, wrap and turn, k4, knit wrap together with next stitch, k4.

Round 8: Knit wrap together with 1st stitch, k3, wrap and turn, p2, wrap and turn, k2, knit wrap together with the stitch, k5.

Round 9: K1, knit wrap together with next stitch, k8.

Rounds 10–12: Knit.

Round 13: *K2tog; repeat from * to end of round—5 stitches.

Cut yarn and thread through remaining 5 stitches with blunt-end needle. Weave in end, leaving cast-on tail for finishing.

FINISH TURTLE HAT

Stuff the Head, Tail, and Back Legs with polyester fiberfill. Stuff Front Flippers, but leave the flipper end flat. For each piece, thread the

holding it until it dries. Glue the tail to the other end next.

Note: Tail for Newborn and Medium sizes is glued just below the center back scallop. Tail for Small and Large sizes is glued between the 2 center back scallops.

Hot-glue the finned flippers on either side of head and the back legs on either side of the tail, evenly spaced between the shell scallops. Hot-glue on eyes.

TURTLE BOOTIES (make 2)

With B and using double-pointed needles, knit cast on 16 (20, 24) stitches.

Join to work in the round as follows: K4 (5, 6) on 1st needle, k8 (10, 12) on 2nd needle, k4 (5, 6) on 3rd needle. Using 3rd needle, k4 (5, 6) from 1st needle—8 (10, 12) stitches on each needle.

Knit 14 (19, 24) rounds in stockinette stitch.

HEEL FLAP

Note: The heel flap is worked back and forth in rows over the back needle.

Turn work.

Beginning with a wrong-side row, work 7 rows in stockinette stitch (k on RS, p on WS).

Row 8 (RS): Sl 1 knitwise, k3 (5, 7), skp. Turn work.

cast-on tail onto a blunt-ended needle and hold it with the opening at the base facing you. Sew into the bars of the cast-on edge by inserting needle under the first bar from the outside and pulling yarn through. Continue by inserting the needle under the next bar, tightening as you go, until all of the cast-on bars have been sewn. Pull

yarn to form a nice finished edge on the front of each piece and a flat ledge underneath the base of each piece that will easily attach to the hat. Weave in end.

Stretch the hat over a glass vase. Run a bead of glue around the flat edge of head and glue it between any two turtle shell scallops,

Row 9 (WS): Sl 1 purlwise, p1 (3, 5), p2tog. Turn work.

Row 10: Sl 1 knitwise, k1 (3, 5), skp. Turn work.

Row 11: Sl 1 purlwise, p1 (3, 5), p2tog. Turn work.

Row 12: Sl 1 knitwise, k1 (3, 5), skp. Turn work—3 (5, 7) stitches.

Row 13: Purl.

Row 14: Knit.

GUSSETS

With back needle, pick up 5 stitches from the left side of the heel flap (1 stitch in each knot along the edge).

K8 (10, 12) stitches over the front needle.

With a 3rd needle, pick up 6 stitches along the other side of the heel flap, then k8 (10, 12) from back needle onto this new needle—22 (26, 30) stitches; 8 (10, 12) stitches on front needle and 14 (16, 18) stitches on back needle.

Round 1: Knit.

Round 2: Knit across front needle, k1, k2tog, knit to last 3 stitches on back needle, k2tog, k1—2 stitches decreased.

Repeat the last 2 rounds twice more—16 (20, 24) stitches; 8 (10, 12) stitches on each needle.

Knit 10 (12, 14) rows.

SHAPE FOOT

Round 1: *K1, k2tog, knit to last 3 stitches, k2tog, k1; repeat from * for back needle—12 (16, 20) stitches; 6 (8, 10) stitches on each needle.

Round 2: Knit.

Repeat last 2 rounds 0 (1, 2) more time(s)—12 stitches; 6 stitches on each needle.

Next round: *K1, k2tog twice, k1; repeat from * for back needle—8 stitches; 4 stitches on each needle.

Cut yarn and thread through remaining 8 stitches with blunt-end needle. Weave in end.

NEWBORN TURTLE HANDSIES (make 2)

With B, knit cast on 16 stitches onto a double-pointed needle and join in the round as for Turtle Booties.

Knit 19 rounds.

Shape foot as for Turtle Booties.

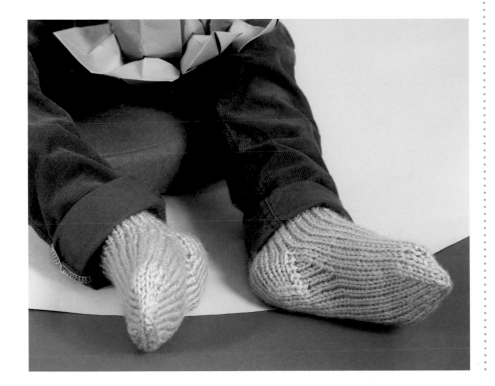

BARNYARD BUDDIES

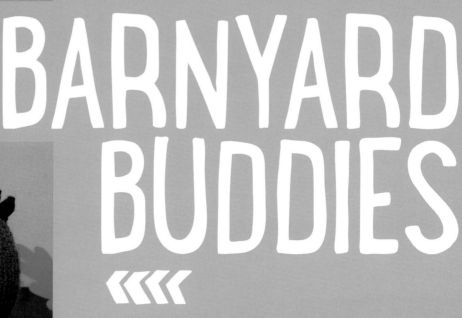

cat
—
chicken
—
bluebird
—
dog
—
duck
—
lamb
—
pig

# cat

I designed this when our beloved Annika joined a soccer team called the Black Cats, made up of girls ages nine to eleven. Hers was such a big hit that I made twenty-four of them for the whole team (and one for the coach's newborn), adding whiskers per her special request. Wanting to make sure they fit them for more than one season, I made most of them in an extra-large size simply by adding 6 more stitches and 4 more rows to the hat. Black cats are my favorite, of course, but I've reknit the project in a light-colored heathered yarn so that you can see the stitches better.

sizes
Newborn (Small, Medium, Large)

finished measurements
13½–16 (15½–18, 17½–20, 19½–22)" (34.5–40.5 [39.5–45.5, 44.5–51, 49.5–56]cm) maximum stretched circumference

gauge
16 stitches and 24 rows = 4" (10cm) in stockinette stitch

materials
For hat: 59 (75, 92, 112) yd (54 [68.5, 84, 102.5]m) / 1 ball Lion Brand Yarn Vanna's Choice, 100% premium acrylic, 3½ oz (100g), 170 yd (156m), in Taupe Mist (A), 17 (17, 23, 23) yd (15.5 [15.5, 21, 21]m) / 1 ball in Linen (B), and ½ (½ , 1, 1) yd (0.5 [1, 1, 1]m) / 1 ball in Soft Pink (C) **(4)**

For hat and booties set: 97 (127, 164, —) yd (88.5 [116, 150, —]m) / 1 ball Lion Brand Yarn Vanna's Choice, 100% premium acrylic, 3½ oz (100g), 170 yd (156m), in Taupe Mist (A), 17 (17, 23, —) yd (15.5 [15.5, 21, —]m) / 1 ball in Linen (B), and ½ (½, 1, 1) yd (0.5 [1, 1, 1]m) / 1 ball in Soft Pink (C) **(4)**

US size 8 (5mm) 16" (40.5cm) circular needle, or size needed to obtain gauge

Set of 5 US size 8 (5mm) double-pointed needles, or size needed to obtain gauge

Stitch marker

Blunt-end yarn needle

Size F-5 (3.75mm) or G-6 (4mm) crochet hook

Styrofoam ball, 1½ (1½, 2, 2)" (3.8 [3.8, 5, 5]cm) in diameter

- Serrated knife
- High-temperature (60-watt) hot-glue gun and glue sticks
- Plastic nose with post, 18mm (18mm, 21mm, 21mm)
- Pink acrylic paint (optional)
- Clear nail polish (optional)
- Round glass bowl vase (see page 19)
- Pair of cat eyes, 18mm
- Scrap of black or dark-brown felt to mount behind the eyes
- 20-gauge black copper wire for whiskers (optional)
- Side-cutting needle-nosed pliers
- Black or dark-brown felt for paw pads on booties and/or handsies (see Felt Templates, page 154)

CAT HAT

With A, make a Rolled-Brim Hat (page 28) or Earflap Hat (page 30)

EARS (make 2)

Lay the finished hat flat. With a crochet hook and starting at the 4th (5th, 6th, 7th) stitch from the center of the top of the hat, pick up 12 (14, 16, 18) stitches. Transfer stitches to a double-pointed needle. Turn hat over to the back side. With a crochet hook, pick up 12 (14, 16, 18) stitches directly behind the stitches on the double-pointed needle—24 (28, 32, 36) stitches total.

Note: You will be working the ears on 2 needles, in the round, knitting the back stitches off the crochet hook on the 1st round (see Picking Up Stitches for Ears, page 21).

Round 1: With A, *ktbl; repeat to end of round.

Round 2: K1, M1, knit to last 2 stitches on front needle, k2tog; k2tog, knit to the last stitch on back needle, M1, k1.

Round 3: Knit to the last 2 stitches on front needle, k2tog; k2tog, knit to the end of round—2 stitches decreased.

Round 4: Repeat round 3—20 (24, 28, 32) stitches; 10 (12, 14, 16) stitches on each needle.

Round 5: Repeat round 2.

Repeat round 3 five (seven, nine, eleven) more times—10 stitches; 5 stitches on each needle.

Next round: *K2tog, k1, k2tog; repeat from * for back needle—6 stitches; 3 stitches on each needle.

Cut yarn and thread through remaining 6 stitches with blunt-end needle. Weave in ends.

CHEEKS

With B and double-pointed needles and leaving a 12" (30.5cm) tail for sewing, cast on 21 (21, 27, 27) stitches.

Beginning with a right-side row, work 8 (8, 12, 12) rows in stockinette stitch (k on RS, p on WS).

Decrease row (RS): *K1, k2tog; repeat from * to the end—14 (14, 18, 18) stitches.

Beginning with a wrong-side row, work 3 rows in stockinette stitch.

To bind off, pass all of the stitches over the 1st stitch until only the 1st stitch remains. Cut yarn, leaving a 6" (15cm) tail for finishing, and thread through the remaining stitch.

FINISH CHEEKS

Cut 2 pieces from the 1½ (1½, 2, 2)" (3.8 [3.8, 5, 5]cm) Styrofoam ball, each ⅛" (3mm) shy of center. Discard the ¼" (6mm) leftover center disk.

Enclose Styrofoam into knit Cheeks, following the directions for Cheeks (page 24).

JAW

With B, using double-pointed needles, and leaving a 12" (30.5cm) tail for finishing, knit cast on 15 (15, 18, 18) stitches.

Knit 1 row.

Join to work in the round as follows: K4 on 1st needle, k6 (6, 9, 9) on 2nd needle, k5 on 3rd needle.

Using 3rd needle, k4 stitches from 1st needle—6 (6, 9, 9) stitches on front needle and 9 stitches on back needle.

Knit 1 row.

Change to C.

Sizes Medium and Large only
Knit 1 row in C.

All sizes
Next round: With C, *K1, k2tog; repeat from * to end of round—10 (10, 12, 12) stitches; 4 (4, 6, 6) stitches on front needle, 6 stitches on back needle.

Next round: *K2tog; repeat from * to end of round—5 (5, 6, 6) stitches; 2 (2, 3, 3) stitches on front needle, 3 stitches on back needle.

Cut yarn and thread through the remaining stitches 5 (5, 6, 6) stitches with blunt-end needle. Weave in end.

NOSE TRIANGLE

With A and double-pointed needles and leaving a 9" (23cm) tail for sewing, knit cast on 24 (24, 32, 32) stitches.

Join to work in the round as follows: K6 (6, 8, 8) on 1st needle, k12 (12, 16, 16) on 2nd needle, k6 (6, 8, 8) on 3rd needle. Using 3rd needle, k6 (6, 8, 8) from 1st needle—12 (12, 16, 16) stitches on each needle.

Round 1: Knit.

Round 2: *K1, k2tog, k to last 3 stitches on needle, k2tog, k1; repeat from * for back needle—20 (20, 28, 28) stitches; 10 (10, 14, 14) stitches on each needle.

Round 3: Knit.

Repeat last 2 rounds 3 (3, 5, 5) more times—8 stitches; 4 stitches on each needle.

Next round: *K1, k2tog, k1; repeat from * to end of round—6 stitches; 3 stitches on each needle.

Cut yarn and thread through the remaining 6 stitches with blunt-end needle. Weave in end.

Follow directions for finishing Nose Triangles (page 24).

WHISKERS (optional)

Cut six 5" (12.5cm) pieces of 20-gauge black copper wire. Poke 3 wire pieces through the cheeks on either side of the plastic nose. With pliers, twist all 6 ends together behind the cheeks and lay the twisted end flat against the back of the cheeks; the Jaw and the Nose Triangle will cover the twisted end when glued on. Curl the tips of the whiskers into closed circles for safety.

FINISH CAT HAT

Hot-glue the nose above the mouth and the knitted Nose Triangle behind the Cheeks, making sure that the triangle bulges in the center. Hot-glue the Jaw behind the Cheeks.

Stretch the hat over a glass vase and hot-glue the Nose Triangle and Cheeks in place. Snip the post off the cat eyes and glue onto an oval-shaped piece of felt (for extra pop) and then glue in place on either side of the Nose Triangle.

CAT BOOTIES (make 2)

With A, follow pattern instructions for Lion Booties (page 93).

NEWBORN CAT HANDSIES (make 2)

With A, follow pattern instructions for Newborn Lion Handsies (page 95).

chicken

This hat actually started out as the Bluebird (page 128). After designing the bird feet, I realized that they would work with any kind of bird at all. I made it in red and called it a cardinal next. Then I came up with the tricolored option, creating these hilarious chickens, originally in white with a red wattle. I made the brown chicken for my great-nephew. He wore it all day long on Thanksgiving, and it looked for all the world like a turkey!

sizes
Newborn (Small, Medium, Large)

finished measurements
13½–16 (15½–18, 17½–20, 19½–22)" (34.5–40.5 [39.5–45.5, 44.5–51, 49.5–56]cm) maximum stretched circumference

gauge
16 stitches and 24 rows = 4" (10cm) in stockinette stitch

materials
For hat: 47 (59, 71, 85) yd (43 [54, 65, 78]m) / 1 ball Lion Brand Yarn Vanna's Choice, 100% premium acrylic, 3½ oz (100g), 170 yd (156m), in White or Toffee (A), 3 (4, 5, 6) yd (2.7 [3.7, 4.6, 5.5]m) in Duckie or Mustard (B), and 6 (7, 8, 9) yd (5.5 [6.4, 7.5, 8.2]m) in Scarlet or Cranberry (C) (4)

For hat and booties set: 47 (59, 71, —) yd (43 [54, 65, —]m) / 1 ball Lion Brand Yarn Vanna's Choice, 100% premium acrylic, 3½ oz (100g), 170 yd (156m), in White or Toffee (A), 39 (56, 77, —) yd (35.5 [51, 70.5, —]m) in Duckie or Mustard (B), and 6 (7, 8, —) yd (5.5 [6.4, 7.5, —]m) in Scarlet or Cranberry (C) (4)

US size 8 (5mm) 16" (40.5cm) circular needle, or size needed to obtain gauge

Set of 5 US size 8 (5mm) double-pointed needles, or size needed to obtain gauge

Stitch marker

Blunt-end yarn needle

Polyester fiberfill

Round glass bowl vase (see page 19)

High-temperature (60-watt) hot-glue gun and glue sticks

Pair of solid black eyes, 9 (9, 12, 12)mm

Side-cutting needle-nosed pliers

CHICKEN HAT

With A, make a Rolled-Brim Hat (page 28) or Earflap Hat (page 30).

BEAK

With B, using double-pointed needles, and leaving a 12" (30.5cm) tail for finishing, knit cast on 24 (28, 32, 36) stitches.

Join to work in the round as follows: K6 (7, 8, 9) on 1st needle, k12 (14, 16, 18) on 2nd needle, and k6 (7, 8, 9) on 3rd needle. Using 3rd needle, k6 (7, 8, 9) from 1st needle—12 (14, 16, 18) stitches on each needle.

Note: The front needle corresponds to the top of the beak.

Round 1: *K1, k2tog, knit to last 3 stitches on needle, k2tog, k1; repeat from * for back needle—20 (24, 28, 32) stitches; 10 (12, 14, 16) stitches on each needle.

Repeat last round 3 (4, 5, 6) times—8 stitches; 4 stitches on each needle.

Next Round: *K1, k2tog, k1; repeat from * for back needle—6 stitches; 3 stitches on each needle.

Cut yarn and thread through the remaining 6 stitches with blunt-end needle. Weave in end.

FINISH BEAK

Sew the Beak following the directions for Beaks and Bills (page 25).

COMB

Note: Comb is worked back and forth in rows.

With C, cast on 2 stitches.

Row 1: K1, kfb—3 stitches.

Row 2: Kfb, k2—4 stitches.

Row 3: K3, kfb—5 stitches.

Row 4: Bind off first 3 stitches, k1—2 stitches.

Repeat these 4 rows 9 (11, 13, 15) times, until you have 10 (12, 14, 16) points. On the last point, bind off all stitches. Cut yarn, leaving a 30 (36, 42, 48)" (76 [91, 106.5, 122]cm) tail for finishing. Fold the knit piece in half and sew up and down the points at the top, making a double-thick Comb. Lightly stuff each point with fiberfill.

WATTLE

Note: The Wattle is worked back and forth in rows.

With C, cast on 2 stitches.

Rows 1–8: Knit.

Row 9: K1, M1, k1—3 stitches.

Row 10: Knit.

Row 11: K1, kfb, k1—4 stitches.

Row 12: Knit.

Row 13: K2, M1, k2—5 stitches.

Row 14: Knit.

Row 15: K2tog, knit to end of row—4 stitches.

Repeat row 15 twice more—2 stitches.

Cut yarn and thread tail through the remaining 2 stitches with blunt-end needle. Weave in end.

FINISH CHICKEN HAT

Stretch the hat over a glass vase. Run a bead of hot glue around the inside edge of the Beak where it will contact the hat and hold it in place until it cools. Glue Wattle under the Beak. Snip posts off the eyes and hot-glue in place.

CHICKEN BOOTIES (make 2)

With B, follow pattern instructions for Owl Booties (page 60).

NEWBORN CHICKEN HANDSIES (make 2)

With B, follow pattern instructions for Newborn Owl Handsies (page 61).

bluebird

This happy little bird captures the spirit of first-time parents. Plus, it is so much fun to work with a primary color. To create a bluebird, use Lion Brand Yarn Vanna's Choice in Sapphire for the main color (A), and Mustard for the beak and feet (B). Follow the instructions for the Chicken (page 124), working the Comb in A, and skip the instructions for the Wattle.

dog

The book *The Fox and the Hound* provided the original model for this perky beagle, but I bet that you could create your own breed (including the family dog) by swapping out the colors and redesigning the ears. The Dog's ears are picked up all across a *row*, unlike most of my other animal hats, so they flop to the side.

sizes

Newborn (Small, Medium, Large)

finished measurements

13½–16 (15½–18, 17½–20, 19½–22)" (34.5–40.5 [39.5–45.5, 44.5–51, 49.5–56]cm) maximum stretched circumference

gauge

16 stitches and 24 rows = 4" (10cm) in stockinette stitch

materials

For hat: 56 (68, 85, 99) yd (51 [62, 78, 90.5]m) / 1 ball Lion Brand Yarn Vanna's Choice, 100% premium acrylic, 3½ oz (100g), 170 yd (156m), in Honey (A), 30 (34, 38, 42) yd (27.5 [31, 34.5, 38.5]m) in Chocolate (B), and 12 (12, 17, 17) yd (11 [11, 15.5, 15.5]m) in White (C) (4)

For hat and booties set: 56 (68, 85, —) yd (51 [62, 78, —]m) / 1 ball Lion Brand Yarn Vanna's Choice, 100% premium acrylic, 3½ oz (100g), 170 yd (156m), in Honey (A), 30 (34, 38, —) yd (27.5 [31, 34.5, —]m) in Chocolate (B), 44 (61, 88, —) yd (40 [56, 80.5, —]m) in White (C) (4)

US size 8 (5mm) 16" (40.5cm) circular needle, or size needed to obtain gauge

Set of 5 US size 8 (5mm) double-pointed needles, or size needed to obtain gauge

Stitch marker

Blunt-end yarn needle

Size F-5 (3.75mm) or G-6 (4mm) crochet hook

Styrofoam ball, 1½ (1½, 2, 2)" (3.8 [3.8, 5, 5]cm)

Serrated knife

High-temperature (60-watt) hot-glue gun and glue sticks

Black plastic nose with post, 18 (18, 21, 21)mm

Scrap of red or burgundy felt for tongue

Polyester fiberfill

Round glass bowl vase (see page 19)

Pair of animal eyes, 20mm

Side-cutting needle-nosed pliers

Scrap of dark-brown felt for paw pads on booties

DOG HAT

With A, knit a Rolled-Brim Hat (page 28) or Earflap Hat (page 30).

EARS (make 2)

Lay the finished hat flat. With a crochet hook and B, starting at the 4th (5th, 6th, 7th) stitch from the center of the top of the hat, pick up 1 stitch. Continuing to work across the *row,* pick up 4 more stitches. Transfer these 5 stitches to a double-pointed needle. Turn hat over to the back side. With a crochet hook, pick up 5 stitches in the row *below* the one where you picked up stitches on the double-pointed needle—10 stitches total.

Note: You will be working the ears on 2 needles, in the round, knitting the back stitches off the crochet hook on the 1st round (see page 21).

Round 1: *Ktbl; repeat from * to end of round.

Rounds 2–5: Knit.

Round 6: *K2, M1, k3; repeat from * for back needle—12 stitches; 6 stitches on each needle.

Rounds 7 and 8: Knit.

Round 9: *K3, M1, k3; repeat from * for back needle—14 stitches; 7 stitches on each needle.

Rounds 10 and 11: Knit.

Round 12: *K3, M1, k4; repeat from * for back needle—16 stitches; 8 stitches on each needle.

Rounds 13 and 14: Knit.

Round 15: *K4, M1, k4; repeat from * for back needle—18 stitches; 9 stitches on each needle.

Rounds 16 and 17: Knit.

Round 18: *K4, M1, k5; repeat from * for back needle—20 stitches; 10 stitches on each needle.

Rounds 19 and 20: Knit.

Round 21: *K5, M1, k5; repeat from * for back needle—22 stitches; 11 stitches on each needle.

Rounds 22–23: Knit.

Round 24: *K5, M1, k6; repeat from * for back needle—24 stitches; 12 stitches on each needle.

Round 25: Knit.

Round 26: *K6, M1, k6; repeat from * for back needle—26 stitches; 13 stitches on each needle.

Round 27: Knit.

Rounds 28: *K6, M1, k7; repeat from * for back needle—28 stitches; 14 stitches on each needle.

Round 29: Knit.

Continue in this pattern, increasing 1 stitch in the middle of each needle, followed by a knit row, 0 (1, 2, 3) more times—28 (30, 32, 34) stitches; 14 (15, 16, 17) stitches on each needle.

Next round: *K1, k2tog, knit to last 3 stitches on needle, k2tog, k1; repeat from * for back needle—24 (26, 28, 30) stitches; 12 (13, 14, 15) stitches on each needle.

Repeat last round 4 (4, 5, 5) more times—8 (10, 8, 10) stitches; 4 (5, 4, 5) stitches on each needle.

Cut yarn, and thread through the remaining stitches with blunt-end needle. Weave in ends.

CHEEKS

With a double-pointed needle and leaving a 12" (30.5cm) tail for finishing, cast on 21 (21, 27, 27) stitches.

Beginning with a right-side row, work 8 (8, 12, 12) rows in stockinette stitch (knit on RS, purl on WS).

Decrease row (RS): *K1, k2tog; repeat from * to end of row—14 (14, 18, 18) stitches.

Beginning with a wrong-side row, work 3 rows in stockinette stitch.

To bind off, pass all of the stitches over the 1st stitch until only the 1st stitch remains. Cut yarn, leaving a 6" (15cm) tail for finishing, and thread through the remaining stitch.

FINISH CHEEKS

Cut 2 pieces from the 1½ (1½, 2, 2)" (3.8 [3.8, 5, 5]cm) Styrofoam ball, each ⅛" (3mm) shy of center. Discard the ¼" (6mm) leftover center disk.

Enclose Styrofoam into knit Cheeks, following the directions for Cheeks (page 24).

JAW

With B, using double-pointed needles and leaving a 9" (23cm) tail for sewing, knit cast on 18 (18, 24, 24) stitches.

Join to work in the round as follows: K4 (4, 6, 6) on 1st needle, k9 (9, 12, 12) on 2nd needle, k5 (5, 6, 6) on 3rd needle. With 3rd needle, k4 (4, 6, 6) from 1st needle—9 (9, 12, 12) stitches on each needle.

Knit 4 (4, 6, 6) rows.

Next round: *K1, k2tog, repeat from * to end of round—12 (12, 16, 16) stitches; 6 (6, 8, 8) stitches on each needle.

Next round: *K2tog; repeat from * to end of round—6 (6, 8, 8) stitches; 3 (3, 4, 4) stitches on each needle.

Cut yarn and thread through the remaining stitches with blunt-end needle. Weave in end.

Follow directions for finishing Jaws (page 24).

LONG SNOUT

With A, using double-pointed needles and leaving a 12" (30.5cm) tail for sewing, knit cast on 30 (30, 40, 40) stitches.

Knit 1 row.

Join to work in the round as follows: K7 (7, 10, 10) on 1st needle, k15 (15, 20, 20) on 2nd needle, k8 (8, 10, 10) on 3rd needle. With 3rd needle, k7 (7, 10, 10) from 1st needle—15 (15, 20, 20) stitches on each needle.

Knit 4 (4, 5, 5) rounds.

Next round: Purl.

Knit 2 rounds.

Sizes Medium and Large only
Next round: *K2, k2tog; repeat from * to end—30 stitches; 15 stitches on each needle.

Next round: Knit.

All sizes
Next round: *K1, k2tog; repeat from * to end of round—20 stitches; 10 stitches on each needle.

Next round: *K2tog to end of round—10 stitches; 5 stitches on each needle.

Cut yarn and thread through remaining 10 stitches. Weave in end.

With cast-on tail, sew following directions for Long Snouts (page 25).

FINISH SNOUT

Hot-glue the black plastic nose between the Cheeks. Cut a teardrop of black felt and hot-glue it to the Jaw. Hot-glue the Jaw behind the Cheeks. Stuff the Snout and attach the Cheeks and Jaw following directions for Long Snouts (page 25).

FINISH DOG HAT

Stretch the hat over a glass vase and hot-glue the base of the Snout in place.

Snip the post off the animal eyes and glue in place.

Note: If you feel the Snout needs a little more stuffing after it has been attached to the hat, add more fiberfill by rolling small pieces into balls and poking them through from the outside with the tip of a double-pointed needle.

DOG BOOTIES (make 2)

With C, follow pattern instructions for Bear Booties (page 41).

NEWBORN DOG HANDSIES (make 2)

With C, follow pattern instructions for Newborn Bear Handsies (page 42).

duck

Because Vanna's Choice yarn comes in a cheerful color called Duckie, I just had to design this hat! You'll have a lot of yellow yarn left, even if you make the Large size. I use the extra yarn to knit beaks and booties for more Ducks because I love this hat just as much in white with a yellow beak and matching webbed feet.

sizes

Newborn (Small, Medium, Large)

finished measurements

13½–16 (15½–18, 17½–20, 19½–22)" (34.5–40.5 [39.5–45.5, 44.5–51, 49.5–56]cm) maximum stretched circumference

gauge

16 stitches and 24 rows = 4" (10cm) in stockinette stitch

materials

For hat: 51 (63, 75, 89) yd (46.5 [57.5, 68.5, 81.5]m) / 1 ball Lion Brand Yarn Vanna's Choice, 100% premium acrylic, 3½ oz (100g), 170 yd (156m), in Duckie (A), and 8 (9, 10, 11) yd (7.5 [8.2, 9, 10]m) in Terracotta (B) 🔢

For hat and booties set: 51 (63, 75, —) yd (46.6 [57.5, 68.6, —]m) / 1 ball Lion Brand Yarn Vanna's Choice, 100% premium acrylic, 3½ oz (100g), 170 yd (156m), in Duckie (A), 47 (63, 83, —) yd (43 [57.5, 76 —]m) in Terracotta (B) 🔢

US size 8 (5mm) 16" (40.5cm) circular needle, or size needed to obtain gauge

Set of 5 US size 8 (5mm) double-pointed needles, or size needed to obtain gauge

Stitch marker

Blunt-end yarn needle

Size F-5 (3.75mm) or G-6 (4mm) crochet hook

Round glass bowl vase (see page 19)

Pair of solid black eyes, 9 (12, 12, 12)mm

Side-cutting needle-nosed pliers

High-temperature (60-watt) hot-glue gun and glue sticks

DUCK HAT

With A, knit a Rolled-Brim Hat (page 28) or Earflap Hat (page 30).

BILL

With B, using double-pointed needle and leaving a 12" (30.5cm) tail for finishing, knit cast on 32 (34, 36, 38) stitches.

Join to work in the round as follows: K8 (8, 9, 9) on 1st needle, k16 (17, 18, 19) on 2nd needle, and k8 (8, 9, 9) on 3rd needle. Using 3rd needle, k8 (8, 9, 9) from 1st needle—16 (17, 18, 19) stitches on each needle.

Note: The front needle corresponds to the top of the Bill.

Knit 4 (5, 5, 5) rounds.

Decrease round: *K1, k2tog, knit to last 3 stitches on needle, k2tog, k1; repeat from * for back needle—28 (30, 32, 34) stitches; 14 (15, 16, 17) stitches on each needle.

Repeat decrease round once (once, twice, twice) more—24 (26, 24, 26) stitches; 12 (13, 12, 13) stitches on each needle.

Next round: *K1, K2tog twice, knit to last 5 stitches on needle, k2tog twice, k1; repeat from * for back needle—16 (18, 16, 18) stitches; 8 (9, 8, 9) stitches on each needle.

Next round: *K1, k2tog, k2 (3, 2, 3), k2tog, k1; repeat from * to end of round—12 (14, 12, 14) stitches; 6 (7, 6, 7) stitches on each needle.

Cut yarn. Thread onto a blunt-end needle and through the remaining 6 (7, 6, 7) stitches. Weave in end.

FINISH BILL

Sew the Bill following the directions for Beaks and Bills (page 25).

TUFT

Cut 30 strands of yarn A, 3–4" (7.5–10cm) long.

With a crochet hook, attach strands of yarn by folding them in half and attaching them around the center top of the hat, as for making fringe. (Pull the loop of the folded strand through a knit stitch on the hat, and then draw the two ends through the loop.) Trim to the desired length.

FINISH DUCK HAT

Stretch the hat over a glass vase. Run a bead of hot glue around the center of the Bill where the prominent ridges will contact the hat, and hold it in place until it cools. Glue each side of the Bill separately to ensure a wide, flat finish.

Snip posts off the eyes and hot-glue in place.

DUCK BOOTIES (make 2)

With B, follow pattern instructions for Toad Booties (page 71).

NEWBORN DUCK HANDSIES (make 2)

With B, follow pattern instructions for Newborn Toad Handsies (page 73).

lamb

Even if you are only planning on making a Newborn set, I highly recommend that you buy two balls of yarn because you're going to be so proud of this hat that you'll want to make another. It uses a shorter version of the highly addictive loop stitch that helps create the Lion's shaggy mane (see page 88). For a girl born at Easter time, I love to make this Lamb in white with a girly pink nose and face and hooves in Silver Grey.

sizes
Newborn (Small, Medium, Large)

finished measurements
13½–16 (15½–18, 17½–20, 19½–22)" (34.5–40.5 [39.5–45.5, 44.5–51, 49.5–56]cm) maximum stretched circumference

gauge
16 stitches and 24 rows = 4" (10cm) in stockinette stitch

materials
For hat: 101 (128, 169, 204) yd (92.5 [117, 154.5, 186.5]m) / 1 (1, 1, 2) balls Lion Brand Yarn Vanna's Choice, 100% premium acrylic, 3½ oz (100g), 170 yd (156m), in Lamb (4)

For hat and booties set: 132 (184, 234, —) yd (120.5 [168.5, 215, —]m) / 1 (2, 2, —) balls Lion Brand Yarn Vanna's Choice, 100% premium acrylic, 3½ oz (100g), 170 yd (156m), in Lamb (A) and 5 (6, 7) yd (4.5 [5.5, 6.5]m) in Black (B) (4)

US size 8 (5mm) 16" (40.5cm) circular needle, or size needed to obtain gauge

Set of 5 US size 8 (5mm) double-pointed needles, or size needed to obtain gauge

Stitch marker

Blunt-end yarn needle

Styrofoam ball, 2 (2, 2½, 2½)" (5 [5, 6.5, 6.5]cm) in diameter

Serrated knife

Scrap amount of black yarn for mouth

High-temperature (60-watt) hot-glue gun and glue sticks

Black plastic nose with post, 18 (18, 21, 21)mm

Round glass bowl vase (see page 19)

Pair of solid black eyes, 9 (12, 12, 12)mm

Side-cutting needle-nosed pliers

Stitch holder (or large safety pin) for booties

SPECIAL STITCHES

Single-Loop Knit

Knit the next stitch, leaving it on the needle. Bring yarn forward between needles. Place your right thumb on the right needle and wrap the yarn over and around your thumb once.

With thumb still wrapped, move yarn back between needles and knit into the same stitch as before, this time dropping it off as usual—2 stitches on right needle.

Pass 1st stitch over 2nd stitch, leaving 1 stitch to lock loop in place.

SLk2tog

Knit 2 stitches together while making a single loop.

LAMB HAT

Knit cast on 54 (60, 66, 72) stitches.

Row 1: Purl.

Place marker and join to work in the round, being careful not to twist stitches.

Round 1: Knit.

Round 2: Purl.

Round 3: *Single-loop knit 7 (8, 9, 10), SLk2tog; repeat from * to end of round—48 (54, 60, 66) stitches.

Round 4: Knit.

Round 5: Single-loop knit to end of round.

Round 6: Knit.

Repeat last 2 rounds 0 (1, 2, 4) more times.

SHAPE FACE OPENING

Round 1: Single-loop knit 5 (6, 7, 7) stitches, k12 (10, 9, 9), single-loop knit to end of round.

Round 2 and all even rounds: Knit.

Round 3: Single-loop knit 4 (5, 6, 6) stitches, k13 (12, 10, 10), single-loop knit to end of round.

Round 5: Single-loop knit 3 (4, 5, 5) stitches, k15 (13, 12, 12) single-loop knit to end of round.

Round 7: Single-loop knit 2 (3, 4, 4) stitches, k16 (15, 13, 13), single-loop knit to end of round.

Round 9: Single-loop knit 1 (2, 3, 3), k18 (16, 15, 15), single-loop knit to end of round.

Sizes Small (Medium, Large) only

Round 11: Single-loop knit 1 (2, 2) stitches, k18 (16, 16), single-loop knit to end of round.

Sizes Medium and Large only

Round 15: Single-loop knit 1 stitch, K18, single-loop knit to end of round.

SHAPE TOP

Note: Switch to double-pointed needles when necessary.

Round 1: K20, single-loop knit to end of round.

Round 2: *K4, k2tog; repeat from * to end of round—40 (45, 50, 55) stitches.

Round 3: K17, single-loop knit to end of round.

Round 4: Knit.

Round 5: K16, single-loop knit to end of round.

Round 6: *K3, k2tog; repeat from * to end of round—32 (36, 40, 44) stitches.

Round 7: K13, single-loop knit to end of round.

Round 8: *K2, k2tog; repeat from * to end of round—24 (27, 30, 33) stitches.

Round 9: Single-loop knit to end of round.

Round 10: SLk2tog to last 0 (1, 0, 1) stitch, single-loop knit 0 (1, 0, 1)—12 (14, 15, 17) stitches.

Round 11: SLk2tog to last 0 (0, 1, 1) stitch, single-loop knit 0 (0, 1, 1)—6 (7, 8, 9) stitches.

Cut yarn, leaving a tail. With a blunt-end needle, thread tail through remaining 6 (7, 8, 9) stitches. Pull tightly and weave in end.

EARS (make 2)

Note: Ears are made separately and sewn to hat.

Using double-pointed needles and leaving a 12" (30.5cm) tail for sewing, knit cast on 12 (12, 14, 14) stitches.

Join to work in the round as follows: K3 on 1st needle, k6 (6, 7, 7) on 2nd needle, k3 (3, 4, 4) on 3rd needle. Using 3rd needle, k3 from 1st needle—6 (6, 7, 7) stitches on each needle.

Rounds 1 and 2: Knit.

Round 3: *K3, M1, k3 (3, 4, 4); repeat from * for back needle—14 (14, 16, 16) stitches; 7 (7, 8, 8) stitches on each needle.

Rounds 4 and 5: Knit.

Round 6: *K3 (3, 4, 4), M1, k4; repeat from * for back needle—16 (16, 18, 18) stitches; 8 (8, 9, 9) stitches on each needle.

Rounds 7 and 8: Knit.

Round 9: *K4, M1, k4 (4, 5, 5); repeat from * for back needle—18 (18, 20, 20) stitches; 9 (9, 10, 10) stitches on each needle.

Rounds 10 and 11: Knit.

Round 12: *K4 (4, 5, 5), M1, k5; repeat from * for back needle—20 (20, 22, 22) stitches; 10 (10, 11, 11)

stitches on each needle.

Rounds 13 and 14: Knit.

Round 15: *K5, M1, k5 (5, 6, 6); repeat from * for back needle—22 (22, 24, 24) stitches; 11 (11, 12, 12) stitches on each needle.

Rounds 16 and 17: Knit.

Sizes Medium and Large only
Round 18: *K6, M1, k6; repeat from

* for back needle—26 stitches; 13 stitches on each needle.

Rounds 19 and 20: Knit.

All sizes
Next round (decrease round): *K1, k2tog, knit to last 3 stitches on needle, k2tog, k1; repeat from * for back needle—18 (18, 22, 22) stitches; 9 (9, 11, 11) stitches on each needle.

Next round: Knit.

Repeat last 2 rounds once (once, twice, twice) more—14 stitches; 7 stitches on each needle.

Next round: *K1, k2tog, k1, k2tog, k1; repeat from * for back needle—10 stitches; 5 stitches on each needle.

Cut yarn and thread through the remaining 5 stitches with a blunt-end needle. Weave in end.

Thread cast-on tail onto a blunt-end needle, fold each Ear in half, and sew up the first 4 rows. Sew Ears to hat using remaining tails, following the photos.

SNOUT

With double-pointed needles and leaving a 12" (30.5cm) tail for finishing, knit cast on 30 (30, 33, 33) stitches.

Knit 1 row.

Join to work in the round as follows: K6 (6, 7, 7) on 1st needle, k18 on 2nd needle, k6 (6, 8, 8) on 3rd needle. Using 3rd needle, k6 (6, 7, 7) from 1st needle—18 stitches on front needle and 12 (12, 15, 15) stitches on back needle.

Knit 3 (3, 5, 5) rounds.

Round 1: *K1, k2tog; repeat from * to end of round—20 (20, 22, 22) stitches; 12 stitches on front needle, 8 (8, 10, 10) stitches on back needle.

Round 2: Knit.

Round 3: *K2tog; repeat from * to end of round—10 (10, 11, 11) stitches.

Cut yarn and thread through remaining 10 (10, 11, 11) stitches with blunt-end needle. Weave in end.

FINISH SNOUT

Cut the Styrofoam ball in half.

Enclose Styrofoam into knit Snout, following the directions for Simple Snouts (page 23).

FINISH LAMB HAT

Sew the Lamb's mouth, following photo, beginning and ending the line of stitches where the plastic nose will be placed (see Stitching a Mouth, page 22).

With a double-pointed needle, make a hole in the center of the Snout to fit the post on the back of the plastic nose. Hot-glue the nose into and around the hole, making sure that the hot glue bonds the yarn to the back of the nose (see Plastic Animal Noses, page 18).

Stretch the hat over a glass vase and hot-glue the Snout into the face opening. Snip the posts off the eyes and hot-glue in place.

LAMB BOOTIES (make 2)

With double-pointed needles and yarn A, knit cast on 16 (20, 24) stitches.

Join to work in the round as follows: K4 (5, 6) on 1st needle, k8 (10, 12) on 2nd needle, k4 (5, 6) on 3rd needle. Using 3rd needle, k4 (5, 6) from 1st needle—8 (10, 12) stitches on each needle.

Knit 14 (19, 24) rounds.

HEEL FLAP

Note: The heel flap is worked back and forth in rows over the back needle.

Turn work.

Beginning with a wrong-side row, work 7 rows in stockinette stitch (k on RS, p on WS). Row 8 (RS): Sl 1 knitwise, k3 (5, 7), skp. Turn work.

Row 9 (WS): Sl 1 purlwise, p1 (3, 5), p2tog. Turn work.

Row 10: Sl 1 knitwise, k1 (3, 5), skp. Turn work.

Row 11: Sl 1 purlwise, p1 (3, 5), p2tog. Turn work.

Row 12: Sl 1 knitwise, k1 (3, 5), skp. Turn work—3 (5, 7) stitches.

Row 13: Purl.

Row 14: Knit.

GUSSETS

With back needle, pick up 5 stitches from the left side of the heel flap (1 stitch in each knot along the edge).

K8 (10, 12) over the front needle.

With a 3rd needle, pick up 6 stitches along the other side of the heel flap, then k8 (10, 12) from back needle onto this new needle—22 (26, 30) stitches; 8 (10, 12) stitches on the front needle and 14 (16, 18) stitches on the back needle.

Round 1: Knit.

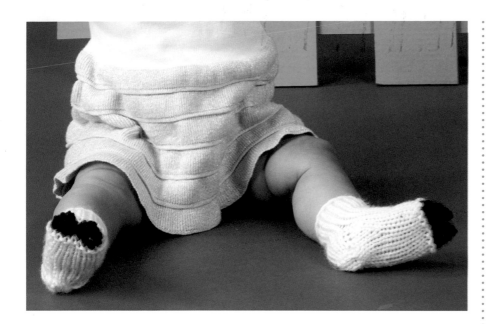

Round 2: Knit across front needle, k1, k2tog, knit to last 3 stitches on back needle, k2tog, k1—2 stitches decreased.

Repeat the last 2 rounds twice more—16 (20, 24) stitches; 8 (10, 12) stitches on each needle.

Knit 9 (11, 15) rounds.

Purl 1 round.

Cut A. Change to B.

Knit 2 rounds.

Sizes Small (Medium) only

Next round: *K2tog, knit to last 2 stitches on needle, k2tog; repeat from * for back needle—16 (20) stitches; 8 (10) stitches on each needle.

Size Medium only

Next round: *K2tog, knit to last 2 stitches on needle, k2tog; repeat from * for back needle—16 stitches; 8 stitches on each needle.

TOES

K4 on front needle, transfer remaining 4 stitches onto stitch holder, transfer 4 stitches from back needle onto stitch holder, k4 stitches of back needle.

Toe 1

Round 1: K2tog, k4, k2tog—6 stitches; 3 stitches on each needle.

Round 2: Knit.

Round 3: *K2tog, k2, k2tog—4 stitches; 2 stitches on each needle.

Round 4: *K2tog; repeat from * to end of round—2 stitches; 1 stitch on each needle.

Cut yarn 30" (76cm) long and thread through remaining 2 stitches with blunt-end needle. Pull tightly and send the needle through the Toe, coming out at the bottom stitch at the front. Sew a few stitches across the gap (see Long Ending Tails, page 22). Use tail for Toe 2.

Toe 2

Slip the first 4 stitches from stitch holder onto needle (back), then slip last 4 stitches from stitch holder onto another needle (front).

Round 1: Knit.

Round 2: K2, k2tog twice, k2—6 stitches; 3 stitches on each needle.

Round 3: Knit.

Round 4: K1, k2tog twice, k1—4 stitches; 2 stitches on each needle.

Round 5: *K2tog; repeat from * to end of round.

Cut yarn and thread through remaining 2 stitches with blunt-end needle. Weave in end.

NEWBORN LAMB HANDSIES (make 2)

With double-pointed needle and yarn A, knit cast on 16 stitches and join in the round as for Lamb Booties.

Knit 18 rounds.

Purl 1 round.

Cut A. Change to B.

Knit 2 rounds.

Make toes as for Lamb Booties.

pig

The entire outfit is worked all in the same color and is so easy to make that you'll marvel at the spectacular reaction this little piggy gets. At ten months old, Sofie wore her hat and booties set to see a parade, and she got more attention from the onlookers than the marching band! The Pig hat has a unique simple snout formed by using a disk-shaped piece of Styrofoam, created by cutting off both ends of the ball and using only the remaining center piece.

sizes

Newborn (Small, Medium, Large)

finished measurements

13½–16 (15½–18, 17½–20, 19½–22)" (34.5–40.5 [39.5–45.5, 44.5–51, 49.5–56]cm) maximum stretched circumference

gauge

16 stitches and 24 rows = 4" (10cm) in stockinette stitch

materials

For hat: 70 (86, 107, 137) yd (64 [78.5, 98, 125.5]m) / 1 ball Lion Brand Yarn Vanna's Choice, 100% premium acrylic, 3½ oz (100g), 170 yd (156m), in Soft Pink (4)

For hat and booties set: 106 (138, 180, —) yd (97 [126, 165, —]m) / 1 (1, 2, —) balls Lion Brand Yarn Vanna's Choice, 100% premium acrylic, 3½ oz (100g), 170 yd (156m), in Soft Pink (4)

US size 8 (5mm) 16" (40.5cm) circular needle, or size needed to obtain gauge

Set of 5 US size 8 (5mm) double-pointed needles, or size needed to obtain gauge

Stitch marker

Blunt-end yarn needle

Size F-5 (3.75mm) or G-6 (4mm) crochet hook

Scrap of gray yarn for nostrils

Styrofoam ball, 2 (2, 2½, 2½)" (5, [5, 6.5, 6.5]cm) in diameter

Serrated knife

Round glass bowl vase (see page 19)

High-temperature (60-watt) hot-glue gun and glue sticks

Pair of solid black eyes, 9 (9, 12, 12)mm

Side-cutting needle-nosed pliers

PIG HAT

Knit a Rolled-Brim Hat (page 28) or Earflap Hat (page 30).

EARS (make 2)

Lay the finished hat flat. With a crochet hook and starting at the 5th (6th, 7th, 8th) stitch from the center of the top of the hat, pick up 6 (8, 10, 12) stitches along top edge of the hat. Transfer stitches to a double-pointed needle. Turn hat over to the back side. With a crochet hook, pick up 6 (8, 10, 12) stitches directly behind the stitches on the double-pointed needle—12 (16, 20, 24) stitches total.

Note: You will be working the Ears on 2 needles, in the round, knitting the back stitches off the crochet hook on the 1st round (see Picking Up Stitches for Ears, page 21).

Round 1: *Ktbl; repeat from * to end of round.

Round 2: *K1, M1, knit to the last stitch on needle, M1, k1; repeat from * for back needle—16 (20, 24, 28) stitches; 8 (10, 12, 14) stitches on each needle.

Round 3: Knit.

Rounds 4 and 5: Repeat Rounds 2 and 3—20 (24, 28, 32) stitches; 10 (12, 14, 16) stitches on each needle.

Round 6: *Knit to last stitch on front needle, M1, k1; k1, M1, knit to end of round—22 (26, 30, 34) stitches; 11 (13, 15, 17) stitches on each needle.

Round 7: *K1, k2tog, knit to last 3 stitches on back needle, k2tog, k1—20 (24, 28, 32) stitches; 10 (12, 14, 16) stitches on each needle.

Round 8: Knit to last 3 stitches on front needle, k2tog, k1; k1, k2tog, knit to end of round—18 (22, 26, 30) stitches; 9 (11, 13, 15) stitches on each needle.

Rounds 9 and 10: Repeat Round 8 twice more—14 (18, 22, 26) stitches; 7 (9, 11, 13) stitches on each needle.

Rounds 11 and 12: Knit.

Round 13: *K1, k2tog, knit to last 3 stitches on front needle, k2tog, k1; repeat from * for back needle—10

(14, 18, 22) stitches; 5 (7, 9, 11) stitches on each needle.

Round 14: Knit.

Sizes Small (Medium, Large) only
Round 15: Knit.

Round 16: *K1, k2tog, knit to last 3 stitches on front needle, k2tog, k1; repeat from * for back needle—10 (14, 18) stitches; 5 (7, 9) stitches on each needle.

Repeat last 2 rounds 0 (1, 2) more time(s)—10 stitches; 5 stitches on each needle.

All sizes

Next round: *K2tog, k1, k2tog; repeat from * for back needle—6 stitches; 3 stitches on each needle.

Cut yarn, leaving 6" (15cm) tail for sewing, and thread through the remaining 6 stitches with a blunt-end needle. Pull tightly and sew a pinch in the tip of the Ear before weaving in end.

SNOUT

With double-pointed needles and leaving a 12" (30.5cm) tail for finishing, knit cast on 24 (24, 30, 30) stitches.

Knit 1 row.

Join to work in the round as follows: K6 (6, 7, 7) on 1st needle, k12 (12, 15, 15) on 2nd needle, k6 (6, 8, 8) on 3rd needle. Using 3rd needle, k6 (6, 7, 7) from 1st needle—12 (12, 15, 15) stitches on front needle and 12 (12, 15, 15) stitches on back needle.

Knit 4 rounds.

Purl 1 round.

Knit 2 (2, 4, 4) rounds.

Next round: *K1, k2tog; repeat from * to end of round—16 (16, 20, 20) stitches; 8 (8, 10, 10) stitches on each needle.

Next round: *K2tog; repeat from * to end of round—8 (8, 10, 10) stitches; 4 (4, 5, 5) stitches on each needle.

Cut yarn and thread through the remaining 8 (8, 10, 10) stitches with blunt-end needle. Weave in end.

FINISH SNOUT

With scrap of gray yarn and blunt-end needle, sew 2 petal-shaped nostrils on the end of the Snout (see box).

Cut the round ends off the Styrofoam ball, leaving a ¾" (2cm) center disk. Enclose ¾" (2cm) Styrofoam disk into knit Snout, following the directions for Simple Snouts (page 23).

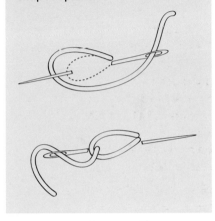

>> The petal-shaped nostrils are created with the classic embroidery stitch known as a lazy daisy. Bring the yarn up through the knitted Snout and make a little loop. Create a small stitch at the top of the loop to hold the petal shape in place.

FINISH PIG HAT

Stretch the hat over a glass vase. Attach the Snout with hot glue, holding it in place until it dries. Snip the posts off the eyes and hot-glue the eyes on.

PIG BOOTIES (make 2)

Follow pattern instructions for Lamb Booties (page 144), working in one color only.

NEWBORN PIG HANDSIES (make 2)

Follow pattern instructions for Newborn Lamb Handsies (page 145) without changing yarn color.

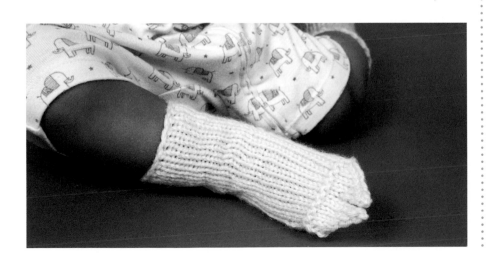

KNITTING ESSENTIALS

If a technique throws you for a loop, just look for it in this section. You can also find helpful video tutorials at www.lionbrand.com.

3-Needle Bind Off

This technique is used to finish the end of web-footed booties and to finish the end of the Panda's ears (page 104). Line up the stitches on your front and back needles, holding the needles parallel to each other. Insert a 3rd needle, as if to knit, into the 1st stitch on both the front and back needles. Knit through both stitches *at the same time*. *Repeat for next pair of stitches on the parallel needles, and then bind off 1 stitch by passing the 1st stitch over the 2nd stitch on the right needle. Repeat from * until all stitches are bound off.

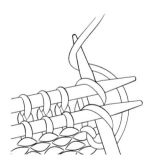

Binding Off

Knit 2 stitches from the left needle. Pass the 1st stitch on the right needle over the 2nd one. *Continue to knit 1 stitch from the left needle, and then pass the previous stitch on the right-hand needle over. Repeat from * until all stitches are bound off and one stitch remains. Cut yarn, leaving a tail, and pull the yarn end through the last stitch.

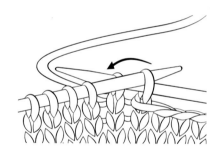

I-cord

This technique produces a cord, or small knitted tube. Cast on the required number of stitches (usually 2 to 4) onto a double-pointed needle. *Knit all the stitches onto a 2nd needle. Slide the stitches to the other end of the 2nd needle—do not turn—and bring the working yarn around the back to begin knitting

again. Repeat from * until I-cord reaches the desired length.

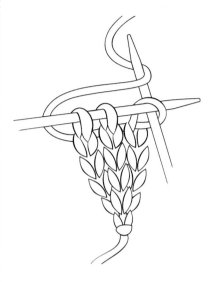

Knit Stitch (k)

Insert right needle, from left to right, into loop on the left needle. Wrap working yarn around the right needle counterclockwise, and then bring right needle through loop. Pull loop off the left needle to create 1 stitch.

Knit 2 Together (k2tog)

Insert needle, from left to right, into 2 loops on the left needle. Wrap working yarn around the right needle counterclockwise, then bring the right needle through both loops. Pull 2 loops off the left needle to decrease by 1 stitch.

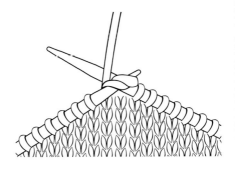

Knit 3 Together (k3tog)

Insert needle, from left to right, into 3 loops on the left needle. Wrap working yarn around the right needle counterclockwise, then bring the right needle through all 3 loops. Pull 3 loops off the left needle to decrease by 2 stitches.

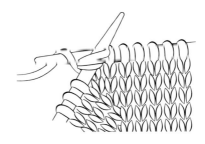

Knit Front & Back (kfb)

Knit into the front leg of the 1st stitch on the left needle. *Without pulling loop from the left needle,* insert needle into the back leg of the same stitch and create a 2nd knit stitch. Pull stitch off left needle to increase by 1 stitch.

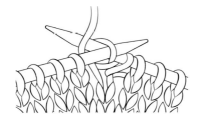

Knit through Back of Loop (ktbl)

Insert right needle, from right to left, into *the back leg* of the loop on the left needle. Wrap working yarn around the right needle counterclockwise, and then bring right needle through loop.

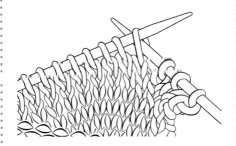

Knitwise

Insert needle, from left to right, as though to knit. The pattern may specify knitwise when slipping stitches or binding off.

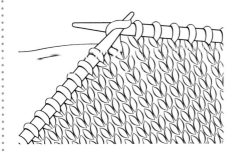

Make 1 (M1)

This invisible increase is created by using the left needle to pick up the horizontal bar between 2 stitches, back to front, and then knitting through the front of the loop.

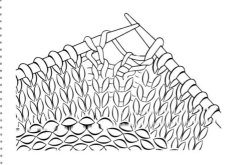

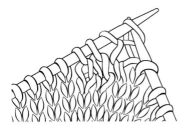

Make 1 Purl (M1P)

This invisible increase is created by using the left needle to pick up the horizontal bar between 2 stitches, back to front.

Then purl through the front of the loop.

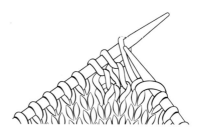

Purl (p)

Insert right needle, from right to left, into loop on the left needle. Wrap working yarn around the right needle counterclockwise, and then bring right needle through loop. Pull loop off the left needle to create 1 stitch.

Purl 2 Together (p2tog)

Insert needle, from right to left, into 2 loops on the left needle. Wrap working yarn around the right needle counterclockwise, then bring the right needle through both loops. Pull 2 loops off the left needle to decrease by 1 stitch.

Purlwise

Insert needle, from right to left, as though to purl. The pattern may specify binding off purlwise, instead of a regular bind off, which is done knitwise.

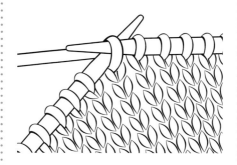

Slip 1 stitch (sl 1)

Insert right needle into next stitch on the left needle, as though to knit, and without working the stitch, simply transfer it onto the right needle.

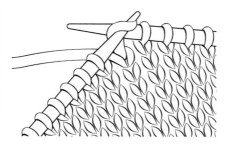

Slip, Knit, Pass Over (skp)

Insert right needle into next stitch on left needle and transfer to the right needle without working the stitch. Knit the next stitch on the left needle.

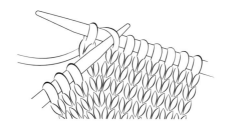

Pass the 1st stitch over the knitted stitch on the right needle to decrease by 1 stitch.

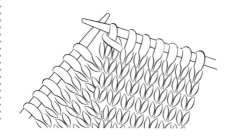

Slip, Slip, Knit (ssk)

Insert right needle knitwise into next stitch on the left needle and transfer it onto the right needle. Repeat with the next stitch on the left needle. Next, insert left needle through the front of the 2 loops on the right needle from left to right. Wrap the working yarn around the right needle counterclockwise, and pull right needle through both slipped stitches. Pull loops off left needle.

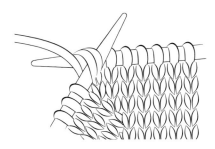

Stranded Color Knitting

To switch between 2 colors in a row, bring the new color underneath the old color, and let the old color drop. Continue knitting with the new color. Repeat for every new color change.

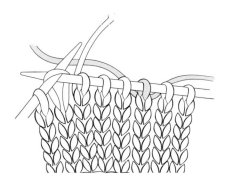

The yarn that is carried over will "float" on the wrong side of the work. Wrap the floats around the working yarn every few stitches.

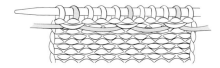

Wrap and Turn

When you reach the point at which the work is to be turned, slip the specified stitch onto the right needle *purlwise*, and then bring the yarn between the needles, to the opposite side of the work (front for a knit row, or back for a purl row).

Transfer the slipped stitch back to the left needle and then return the yarn to its original position to "wrap" the stitch.

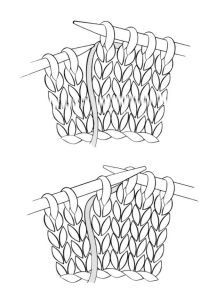

Turn the work and continue working as directed. When you come to the wrapped stitch again, pick up the "wrapped" loop under the next stitch on the left needle and knit or purl it together with the same stitch. Continue working across the row as directed.

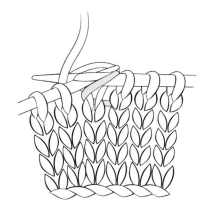

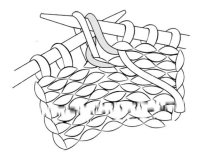

FELT TEMPLATES

Little paws need paw pads! Trace the templates for the bootie or handsie size needed onto a sheet of paper, place the shapes on a piece of felt, and cut around. All templates are shown at actual size, so there's no need to enlarge them.

Newborn

Small

Medium

Large

RESOURCES

Lion Brand Yarn
www.lionbrand.com
135 Kero Road
Carlstadt, NJ 07072
(800) 258-YARN (9276)
Distributor of Vanna's Choice and
Heartland yarns

Jo-Ann Fabrics
and Craft Stores
www.joann.com
5555 Darrow Road
Hudson, OH 44236
(330) 656-2600
For plastic animal noses, eyes, and
Lion Brand yarns

Michaels Craft Center
www.michaels.com
8000 Bent Branch Drive
Irving, TX 75063
(800) MICHAELS (642-4235)
For glass vases, Lion Brand Yarn
Vanna's Choice

ACKNOWLEDGMENTS

Special thanks to three particular family members of the USS *Alabama Blue*: Shalane Itwaru of Little Darlings Photography, in Bremerton, Washington, who gifted me with the first, dazzling professional pictures of Gramminals. And to Jacquelyn Phillips, who dedicated the eleventh and twelfth days of her newborn, Jackson's, life to model for them under her watchful eye. These stunning photos inspired me to take this project seriously and, no doubt, opened many doors along the way to publishing this book.

Many thanks, also, to the good folks at Lion Brand Yarn Company for their enthusiastic encouragement: Pamela Fischbein, who was my point of contact throughout the contest; Zontee Hou, who was the first to say to me, "You should write a book!", Vanna White, who has the most generous spirit and who is even sweeter and lovelier in person than she appears on TV. And most especially to Keith Bobier, my most trusted ally since day one, whose kind and thoughtful guidance, delightful sense of humor, and über-responsiveness kept me on track from beginning to end.

Thanks to my editors at Potter Craft: Betty Wong, who convinced me that it was going to be easy to turn my designs into a book, and Caitlin Harpin, who had the difficult job of doing the real work with me.

And loving gratitude to my aunt, Edda De Martini, who taught me to knit in 1961. That same year, she became a decades-long patron of Danny Thomas' St. Jude Children's Research Hospital, which, it turns out, is Vanna White's favorite charity, too. Auntie Edda and Vanna would both want me to ask you to please use Vanna's Choice yarns, as Lion Brand Yarn Company donates a portion of the purchase price of each skein you buy to St. Jude Children's Research Hospital.

INDEX

Note: Page numbers in *italics* indicate patterns.

31901059317455